21
DAYS TO

Work with
Crystals

Also in the 21 Days series

21
DAYS TO

Work with
Crystals

Crystal Energy for Healing,
Transformation, and Self-Protection

JUDY HALL

HAY HOUSE
Carlsbad, California • New York City
London • Sydney • New Delhi

Published in the United Kingdom by:
Hay House UK Ltd, The Sixth Floor, Watson House,
54 Baker Street, London W1U 7BU
Tel: +44 (0)20 3927 7290; www.hayhouse.co.uk

Published in the United States of America by:
Hay House Inc., PO Box 5100, Carlsbad, CA 92018-5100
Tel: (1) 760 431 7695 or (800) 654 5126; www.hayhouse.com

Published in Australia by:
Hay House Australia Pty Ltd, 18/36 Ralph St, Alexandria NSW 2015
Tel: (61) 2 9669 4299; www.hayhouse.com.au

Published in India by:
Hay House Publishers India, Muskaan Complex,
Plot No.3, B-2, Vasant Kunj, New Delhi 110 070
Tel: (91) 11 4176 1620; www.hayhouse.co.in

A catalogue record for this book is available from the British Library.

Tradepaper ISBN: 978-1-4019-7122-9
E-book ISBN: 978-1-78817-895-2
Audiobook ISBN: 978-1-78817-858-7

Interior illustrations: 2, 7, 39, 93, 145: Shutterstock; 104, 106, 108, 109, 172, 173, 174: Lucy Webster

Printed in the United States of America

10 9 8 7 6 5 4 3 2 1

Contents

Publisher's Note

Research has shown that establishing a habit requires 21 days of practice. That's why Hay House has decided to adapt the work of some of its most prestigious authors into these short, 21-day courses, designed specifically to develop new mastery of subjects such as discovering the power of crystals.

Other titles that will help you to explore further the concepts featured in this 21-day program are listed at the beginning of this book.

21 Days to Work with Crystals draws from Judy Hall's *Crystals Made Easy* (Hay House, 2018), previously published as *Crystals (Hay House Basics)* (Hay House, 2015).

Introduction

Powerful, potent, and therapeutic, crystals have many uses. What excites me is that crystals adapt themselves and reveal new possibilities the more we allow them to show us what they can do. Over the next 21 days we're going to explore both traditional and innovative applications for these potent beings—I call them "beings" because, as you'll discover, crystals actively engage with you. They are sentient, with enormous intelligence and focused intent.

I could have taken a "cook-book" approach to this program, saying "this crystal is good for this" and "that one is good for that." Of course, that would be true, but you could go to my other books for such information. (I'll steer you in the right direction in the Resources at the end of the book—although this is not strictly necessary, as you'll discover the properties of the crystals as you work with them.)

In this book we'll look each day at a different aspect of crystals, so you build skills that you can use across a variety of applications. Every day I've included a practical exercise to expand your sensitivity to crystal energy and help you explore its potential. In 21 days you will have tasted a wide spectrum of crystal possibilities.

We'll look at specific crystals, some old some new, basic and advanced, earthy and of high vibration, so that no matter whether you're a complete beginner or an experienced crystal worker, you'll find something here to inspire and excite you. Many of the crystals I mention can be viewed in color on the corresponding downloadable PDF. (*See page 193 for instructions on how to access this bonus content*).

Today and tomorrow we'll start by covering some essential crystal basics: Finding your crystals and keeping them working for you. Please don't skip these days or you'll be disappointed with your crystal results. A little time spent now will repay you with the most potent crystal energies.

Crystal blessings,

Judy Hall

DAY 1

Finding Your Crystals

What we are going to do today is find *your* crystals—the ones that interact to optimum effect with *your* energies. You have a unique energy frequency and the secret to effective crystal working is to find the crystals that respond to it. You may like to set aside a whole day for this process, especially if you are going to learn how to dowse for your crystals, but there is one simple step that enables you to find your crystals quickly—this is to open the chakras in the palms of your hands.

The Palm Chakras

To open your palm chakras, open and close your hands into fists several times. Then bring your hands together so that the palms touch, open your hands slightly, and bring them back together again. It will feel like a ball of energy builds up between your palms, which may start to tingle. Always open these chakras before choosing or working with a crystal.

Opening the Palm Chakras

Let Your Crystal Find You

Everyone who is interested in crystals—and especially people who were indifferent before they were befriended by a crystal—has had the experience of a crystal "winking" at them. You go into a store or you trawl the internet, and a crystal catches your eye. This is the one for you. It is not necessarily the biggest, the prettiest, or the priciest stone. It may be a raw lump, or it may be tumbled or faceted. But it is the most potent crystal for *you*.

So, rather than looking up the meaning of a crystal, or seeking a crystal for a particular symptom or application, try a different approach. Visit a store that sells crystals and see what calls to you, or look at what you have in your collection already. These eager beings have been longing to work with you. Now is the time. You can also let the crystals on the download call to you or look at them online.

Keep a note of the crystals that choose you and record your immediate intuitions about how they want to work with you, and any insights that develop later.

Exercise: The Power of Touch

1. Open your palm chakras.

2. If you already have a selection of crystals, place them on a table. Close your eyes and, if the stones are not too delicate, gently move them around. With your eyes still closed, move your hand over the crystals in a circular motion until one pulls your hand toward it or you feel a tingle in your palm. If nothing happens, try your other

hand or go to Day 2 to learn how to purify your crystals and then try again.

3. Alternatively, if you're in a crystal store and nothing immediately jumps out at you, open your palm chakras and run your fingers through the tubs of crystals. One will stick to your fingers or feel particularly good in your hand. This is *your* crystal. Next, pick up a larger crystal and compare how you feel. If you find you can't put a stone down, that's the crystal for you. Please note that some crystals may require a thorough cleansing, see Day 2, before you feel fully attuned to them.

Exercise Your Intuition

If you have a crystal collection, you have already exercised your intuition in picking them (or they selected you). Simply look at your collection with softly focused eyes and see which one winks at you, or open your palm chakras and let your fingers intuitively pick one up. Hold it gently to connect to its energies. However, it may need purifying and activating so you may need to refer to Day 2.

Or, walk into a crystal store and let yourself be pulled in a particular direction rather than thinking about where to go. See which crystal catches your eye. Again, you may need to take it home and purify it before working with it, as crystals pick up the energy of everyone who has handled them.

The internet is a great tool for crystal selection from the comfort of your home. Log on to one of the sites listed in the Resources (*see page 187*) or to your favourite crystal site, preferably one that shows you several photographs of the same type of crystal. Then, look at the screen with half-closed eyes and run through the pictures until one catches your eye. Once your crystal has called to you, purchase it.

Finally, if you have books on crystals, flick through the pictures or let the pages fall open randomly at a particular entry. While your eyes are softly focused, ask the crystal to connect more strongly with you so that you sense its energy—the illustrations on the download are particularly useful, as are those in my book *101 Power Crystals*, in which John van Rees Jr. really captured the energy of the crystals in his remarkable photographs.

Exercise: Dowsing

Dowsing is an excellent way to choose your crystal. There are two methods: One with a pendulum and one using your fingers.

To use a pendulum you need to establish movements representing "yes," "no," and "maybe." I find the easiest method is to hold the pendulum loosely with the chain wrapped around my fingers and anchored lightly with my thumb, with about a hand's breadth of chain hanging down. Experiment with what works best for you—some people simply hold it between their thumb and forefinger.

1. Hold the pendulum over your knee and ask "Is my name [give your real name]?" The pendulum will move of its own volition either circling or swinging from side to side. Note which way it swings as this is your "yes" answer.

2. Then give a false name and this gives your "no" answer—it will swing in another direction.

3. Next, mix your first name with a false surname to get a "don't know/maybe" answer. For me this is a kind of shimmy of the pendulum without much movement.

4. Once you know your "yes" and "no" indications, hold the pendulum over a crystal and ask "Is this the right crystal

for me?" If the answer is a rather half-hearted "yes" or a "maybe," ask "Is there a better one?" If the answer is "yes," check out whether the better one is another crystal of the same type or a different one.

5. Alternatively, to finger dowse simply loop your forefinger and thumb of one hand together. Through the loop link the forefinger and thumb of your other hand. As you ask your question, pull gently. If the answer is "yes," the loop will hold. If the answer is "no," your hands will pull apart easily.

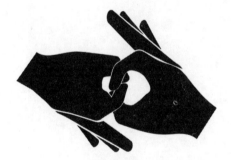

Finger Dowsing

DAY 2

Preparing Your Crystals

Today's Crystals

Your crystal collection

Today you are going to learn how to prepare your crystals for use, as there are a few essential steps that precede attuning to your crystals. Please don't miss them out and rush on to what you feel is the interesting bit. These steps are vital if you are to fully harness the power of your stones. As crystals rapidly absorb negative energies and pick up the vibes of everyone who handles them, they need to be kept purified and to be activated so that they work to their fullest potential.

People often say, "Crystals don't work for me," and when I respond, "But have you asked them to?" they are surprised. Asking your crystals to work with you for your highest good—and that of others—amps up crystal power enormously.

I like to have a regular crystal cleansing day, when I spray all the crystals in my house with Clear 2 Light (a proprietary crystal cleanser and recharger from Petaltone Essences) and put them outside to recharge in the sunlight or moonlight. In my case that's quite a task as I have a huge collection of crystals, but I treat the cleansing time as a meditation and healing day for myself.

Cleansing Your Crystal

This is a fundamental rule of working with crystals. No matter whether you're working with a favorite crystal you've had for a long time or one you've just bought home from a store, *you must cleanse it before use.*

If your crystal is tumbled or robustly formed, simply hold it under running water for a few minutes, carefully immerse it in a stream or the sea, or use a proprietary crystal cleanser.

However, if the crystal is delicate, layered, or friable, place it in brown rice overnight, pass it through the light of a candle or the smoke from a smudge stick, or use a proprietary cleanser.

Pop it in the sunlight or moonlight to recharge its batteries. Or use a proprietary crystal recharger—one drop or a quick spray and it is done. (To make a spray bottle, put seven drops of the crystal cleanser into pure spring water. You can add essential oils or vodka as a preservative, but the spray will keep for several days without any).

Remember:

- Do not blow on crystals to cleanse them, as your energies may not be pure.

- Salt water can damage delicate crystals, especially those with many points or layers, or those growing from a bed, as it may force them apart. So use it with care.

Crystals benefit from regular cleansing and recharging. Having a monthly "crystal day" when you purify the crystals and then put them out into the sunlight or moonlight to recharge helps you to attune more closely with your crystals and raises your own energies, too. You can also meditate with your crystals to see if they have anything to share with you (*see Day 21*).

Exercise:
Feel the Difference

1. Hold an uncleansed crystal for a few moments and make a note of what you feel.

2. Cleanse your crystal. Then, hold it, and notice the changes.

Ask Your Crystal to Work with You

Crystals are very wise beings who see much further than we mere mortals, but if you don't ask one to work with you, how will it know what you want it to do? Having said that, I try not to be too specific as I feel it restricts the crystal if I only ask from my limited Earth-perspective vision. I ask for the crystal to work for my highest good and that of other people, and to do what is appropriate for my spiritual growth and add "this or something better" or "as appropriate" to requests. There are times when I feel stuck in a situation I'd much rather get out of, but if there's something I need to learn from it, or a gift I need to gain, scrambling out too quickly may lose me that opportunity.

Therefore, I would rather the crystal supports me as I go through the necessary challenge.

Holding a crystal and focusing on it for a few moments charges it up, filling it with intention. If you have a specific purpose in mind for your crystal, hold it between your hands. Concentrate your thoughts on the crystal and ask that it cooperates with you to fulfill that purpose in the best way possible and attunes to your purpose.

Deprogramming

Once you no longer need a crystal, deprogram it. To do this, cleanse it, then hold it in your hands. Thank it for working on your behalf, but state that the work is now complete. Ask that any program in the crystal is dissolved and that the crystal becomes quiescent until you require it again. However, you may also wish to state that if the crystal is working on your behalf at a higher level than you are aware of, you want it to continue with that work.

Storing your crystals

Keep your crystal(s) in a drawer or a box when not in use. Tumbled crystals can be stored together in a bag—add a Carnelian to keep them energetically purified and cleansed—but delicate crystals need to be wrapped separately. Cleanse them before use. Crystals that are on display need to be cleansed frequently.

DAY 3

Getting to Know Your Crystals: Attuning

Today's Crystals

Any crystal in your collection

Today we are looking at the very important topic of how to attune to your crystals, so that you can work productively with them.

The secret to successfully harnessing crystal power is to find exactly the right crystals to interact with you and then attune to them. Crystals have a subtle but measurable electromagnetic field, and so does the human body. This energy can be transferred between the two, but the field may be affected by the color or shape of the crystal (*see Day 4*) and by your own unique frequency.

If a Crystal Doesn't Feel Right

Not every crystal will suit you, as your individual energy patterns harmonize better with some crystal frequencies than others. It may be that a crystal that causes you discomfort when attuning simply isn't the crystal for you at this time, so try another type. If a crystal feels uncomfortable or unappealing, however, it might be stirring up issues that need addressing later. That's why learning to attune to a crystal quickly helps you to select exactly the right stone for you, rather than picking one that someone else suggests. If the crystal highlights emotional baggage or mental constructs that need shifting, my books (*see Resources*) can help you to research crystals. We'll also be learning to clear our baggage on Days 14 and 16. However, for the time being, work with crystals that feel comfortable.

How Crystals Work

Crystals have a lattice-like orderly internal crystalline structure. The exact structure is unique to each type. These structures create, absorb, anchor, or radiate energy. Color, which we'll explore on Day 5, has a powerful effect. Many black crystals, such as Smoky Quartz for instance, have a structure that captures energy. This means that the crystal holds on to detrimental energies such as electromagnetic "smog," or negative thoughts, and transmutes their toxic effect. They are protective, too. Wearing one keeps you safe, and we'll be looking at protection on Day 6. The color is created by minute traces of other minerals (*see Day 5*) and we'll explore shape tomorrow. Crystals take you deep into healing theta brainwave states and also carry powerful bioscalar waves—we'll be coming on to that on Day 10!

Exercise:
Harmonizing with Your Crystal

When you become the keeper of a new crystal, always take time to attune to it.

1. Open the palm chakras and sit quietly holding your crystal in your hands.

2. Breathe gently and focus your attention on the crystal. Ask that your stone works with you in love and truth for your highest good. Half close your eyes and simply

gaze at your crystal. Ask it to communicate in the most appropriate way for you.

3. Continue to breathe gently and be receptive to the response, which may come in the form of a bodily sensation, a feeling, or an intuition.

4. After a few minutes notice how you feel. Are you calm and relaxed, or twitchy and jittery? Is an emotion rising? Does a particular part of your body tingle or ache? Is one of your chakras lighting up—becoming hot, energized, and active, possibly fluttering, tingling, and fizzing? *(You'll find a diagram of the major chakras on page 39 if you are unfamiliar with the location of them.)*

5. Move your crystal around your body to check out sensations and intuitions. If it feels good to keep it in a particular place, leave it there for a while. Don't force anything; simply go with what feels right. Let the crystal be your guide.

6. Ask yourself if your crystal is dropping thoughts into your mind. If so, trust the process. Or has your stone found another way to communicate, for example, through bodily or intuitive sensation? Remember, crystals are creative beings.

7. After five minutes or so thank the crystal for its work, put it to one side, and consciously disconnect your attention from it—unless your intuition tells you to keep it in your pocket or somewhere close by.

8. Repeat steps 1 to 7 with your other crystals.

Record Your Experience

Write down all that you remember from an attunement session in a notebook. Record the date and time, the moon phase (dark, new, waxing, waning, or full,) your mood before you started, the type of crystal, what you experienced, and how you feel afterward. This not only helps you keep track of the effect that different crystals have, but it also charts whether you are more sensitive to crystal energies at particular times—for instance the moon cycle can affect your sensitivity, as can the time of day.

DAY 4

Getting to Know Your Crystals: Type and Shape

Today's Crystals

Amethyst, Citrine, Clear Quartz, Rose Quartz, Smoky Quartz, Snow Quartz

Our focus today is on learning about different types and shapes of crystals. Some stones are shining, glamorous, and expensive. Others are rough and seemingly dull—until you connect to their power. Many crystals are tumbled, cut, or faceted to enhance their appearance, but work just as well in their natural form. However, their external shape can alter how their energy is experienced. Some crystals are found in one color only; others come in several. And color, as with shape, subtly changes the way crystals work (*see Day 5*). All crystals generate, store, regulate, transmit, and absorb energy

Exercise:
Sensing the Difference

For this exercise you need a variety of crystal types: Points, shaped, or raw stones, and tumbled crystals. I suggest using Amethyst, Citrine, Clear Quartz, Rose Quartz, Smoky Quartz, and Snow Quartz, which are all types of Quartz but which differ subtly in their energetic emanations.

1. Lay out the crystals in two separate columns on a neutral background, the tumbled on the left and the points, shaped, or raw stones on the right side pointing toward you, about two fingers' width apart.

2. Open the chakras in your palms.

3. With your palms facing down, run each hand in turn down the left-hand column (the tumbled stones) to ascertain your most receptive hand. Your palm may tingle or feel hot or cold.

4. Now with your eyes closed, run your receptive hand down the column again, letting yourself feel the energy radiating from the crystals. Don't try to *do* anything with

your mind, just allow yourself to *feel* the energy through your hands. Then look at and feel the energy of each crystal in turn, telling yourself, "This is what Snow Quartz feels like," and so on. With a little practice you'll soon be able to feel how the basic Quartz energy changes according to the specific type of crystal. For example, Snow Quartz has a much slower frequency than Clear Quartz, and Citrine positively fizzes.

5. Once you've become familiar with the tumbled crystals, turn your attention to the points and shapes. Points focus energy toward you when the point is facing you, and channel it away when the point faces outward.

6. Put each point in turn on your receptive hand, first pointing it up your arm and then toward your fingers. Notice the difference this makes.

7. Next, you can move on to putting the point above your head. Point it downward first and then point it upward. Then do the same, keeping the crystal below your feet, first pointing it "up" toward the feet, then "down" away from the feet.

When you've had some practice, you may like to experiment with other crystal shapes or repeat the exercise with different shapes of the same crystal.

The Effect of External Shape

Although the internal lattice of a crystal, which is not visible to the naked eye, is fundamental to crystal energy, the external shape has a bearing, too. Such shapes may be natural or artificially cut.

- **Ball:** Its rounded shape emits energy equally all round; a window to move through time.

- **Cluster:** Several points on a base radiate energy in all directions equally.

- **Double terminated:** Points at both ends emit energy in two directions; breaks old patterns.

- **Egg:** Its gently rounded end focuses and discharges energy.

- **Elestial:** Folded crystal with many terminations, windows, and inner planes, which radiates flowing energy; absorbs and transmutes negative vibes; opens you up to insights and change.

- **Generator:** Single, six-pointed termination or several points radiating in all directions; focuses healing energy or intention; draws people together; attracts abundance.

- **Geode:** Rough outside, beauty and strength within; its "cave-like" formation amplifies, conserves, and slowly releases energy.

- **Phantom:** Enclosed, pointed inner pyramid, which breaks old patterns and raises vibrations.

- **Point:** Faceted termination; pointing it away from the body draws off energy; pointing it toward the body draws in energy; cleansing and energizing.

- **Square:** Consolidates energy; anchors intention and grounds it; draws off negative energy and transforms it.

- **Sceptre:** A "head" formed around a central rod; an excellent power and restructuring tool.

- **Twin:** Two crystals usually of equal length sharing a base; draws people together.

- **Wand:** A long point or a crystal specially shaped to resemble a wand; focuses energy and draws in energy (if you point it toward yourself) or draws it off (if you point the wand away from your body, or pull the wand away and "flick" the energy off).

TODAY'S CRYSTALS

Amethyst

Vibration: High to extremely high, according to type

- Extremely powerful and protective, with strong healing and cleansing powers.

- Guards against psychic attack, transmuting energy.

- Natural tranquilizer.

- Blocks geopathic stress, and negative environmental energies.

- Enhances higher states of consciousness and spiritual awareness.

Citrine

Vibration: High

- A "feel-good" crystal that raises self-esteem.

- Vibrant energizer; powerful cleanser and regenerator.

- Stone of prosperity and abundance.

- Warming and highly creative.

- Absorbs, transmutes, and dissipates toxic energy or conflict.

- Protective for the environment.

~

Clear Quartz

Vibration: Can be high, according to type

- Energy enhancer and powerful healer.

- Soothes and protects.

- Repairs and replenishes the aura.

- Radiates energy into the environment or the body.

- Stimulates the immune system and regulates physical and mental energy.

- Deep cleanser on both physical and soul levels.

- Dissolves karmic seeds (blockages and issues from the past—in this and other lives—that lodge in the energy body and, if not dealt with, can manifest themselves as physical disorders).

- Amplifies intuition.

~

Rose Quartz
Vibration: High

- Gentle and loving.

- Perfect heart-healer and emotional nourisher.

- Excellent for de-stressing, soothing, and stabilizing.

- Purifies and supports forgiveness.

- Teaches how to love and value yourself.

~

Smoky Quartz
Vibration: Earthy to high, according to type

- Efficient for grounding and cleansing.

- Protective.

- Blocks geopathic stress and electromagnetic smog.

- Assists elimination and detoxification.

- Teaches how to leave behind anything that no longer serves.

～

Snow Quartz
Vibration: Earthy

- Gentle; healing; purifying; revitalizing; calming.

- Energizes the soul and connects to your true self.

- Essential component in ancient stone circles, tombs, and megalithic portals that connect to the stars and circulate universal energy.

- Enhances psychic abilities and calms the mind.

～

DAY 5

Crystals and Color

Today's Crystals

One crystal of each color

Yesterday looked at types and shapes of crystals. Today we're going to delve into another important aspects of crystals—their color.

The colors of a crystal are created by minerals and trace elements. Let's look at some examples. When Hematite is present, the crystals may be red or silver—Hematite is a deep, blood red when raw but it magically transforms into silver when polished. Rutile (titanium) turns Quartz pink to create Rose Quartz, but also presents as the golden or green threads in Rutilated Quartz. Iron stains crystals yellow, whereas Chlorite turns them green, and so on. Colors have specific and general properties, as well as chakra links and associations through which healing is facilitated—we'll be looking at these links tomorrow.

Exercise: Sensing Color

You need: One crystal of each color for this exercise.

1. Lay the crystals out in a rainbow arc of color, starting with black and brown at one end and finishing with white and silver at the other.

2. Open your palm chakras.

3. Run your most receptive hand along the arc of color starting with the black. Let yourself feel the energy change as you move from one color to the next. (Do this with your hand rather than your mind, although you can tell yourself: "This is what black feels like; this is how blue feels" and so on.)

4. When you have done this a few times, close your eyes and let yourself sense which color you have touched. Then open your eyes to check.

5. Now mix up the colors into a swirl and then run your hand over them with your eyes closed.

6. Pick up a crystal and sense what color it is before you open your eyes to check.

How did you get on? Did you find that you were able to sense the color of the crystals with your eyes closed? Don't worry if you find this difficult at first. As with anything, the more you practice this exercise, the easier it will get.

The Crystal Rainbow

Here is a basic guide to the properties of the colors in crystals:

- **Silver-grey:** Metallic with alchemical properties of transmutation; traditionally imparts invisibility, making excellent journeying crystals (*see Day 19*).

- **Black:** Strongly protective and grounding; entraps and transmutes negative energies; an excellent detoxifier, although some, such as Obsidian, work cathartically and need to be used with care.

- **Brown:** Resonates with the earth star chakra (*see Day 6*); strongly cleansing and purifying; grounding and protecting; absorbs toxic emanations and negative energies; induces stability and centeredness.

- **Pink:** Exceedingly gentle, carrying the essence of unconditional love; provides comfort and alleviates anxiety; excellent "first aid" emotional healer; overcomes loss, dispels trauma, and promotes forgiveness and attunement to universal love.

- **Peach:** Gently energizing; unites the heart and sacral chakras, combining love with action.

- **Red:** Resonates with the base and sacral chakras; energizes and activates, strengthening the libido and stimulating creativity; draws off or generates energy as required; traditionally treats blood, hemorrhages, and inflammation.

- **Orange:** Resonates with the sacral chakra; vibrant and vital; stimulates creativity and assertiveness; grounds projects in the physical world.

- **Yellow:** Resonates with the solar plexus chakra and the mind; instils clarity; balances the emotions and the intellect; golden crystals have long been associated with wealth and abundance.

- **Green:** Resonates with the heart chakra; provides emotional healing and activates compassion; calming and cleansing, instilling tranquility.

- **Green-blue and turquoise:** Activates the third eye, uniting heart and intuition; promotes profound peace and relaxation; resonates with higher levels of being, and stimulates spiritual awareness and metaphysical abilities, drawing higher consciousness down to Earth and anchoring it.

- **Blue:** Resonates with the throat, third eye, and soma chakras; stimulates self-expression and assists communication; links to the highest states of consciousness; stimulates intuition and metaphysical abilities, bringing about mystical perception.

- **Lavender/lilac/purple:** Resonates with the soul star and stellar gateway (the higher crown) chakras and multi-dimensional realities; draws spiritual energy into the material plane and opens metaphysical abilities; encourages service to others.

- **White:** Resonates with the higher crown chakras and highest realms of being; powerful energizer, purifies and heals the aura and the physical body; radiates energy out into the environment; carries the vibration of pure light and higher consciousness.

- **Combination and bi-colored:** Creates exciting possibilities; synergizes the qualities of component colors to work holistically. Often more effective than individual parts, the vibrations are raised to a higher energetic frequency.

DAY 6

Crystals and the Chakras

Today's Crystals

Your crystals from Day 5

Today we are turning our attention to the way in which crystals can work with the energy centers in the body known as chakras.

In recent times chakras have often been simplified to seven main energy points on the body but, as ancient chakra diagrams show, there are many more chakras and additional chakras are coming on line as consciousness expands.

We have already connected to the receptive palm chakras, but there is also an essential grounding chakra below your feet—this is the earth chakra or earth star, which you'll need to open. We'll also activate higher chakras on Day 18.

Vortices for the reception or transmission of subtle energy and linkage points between the subtle energy bodies that surround and interpenetrate your physical body, chakras mediate energy flow. They help the body assimilate Qi, the life force, and assist communication between different dimensions of being: Physical, emotional, mental, karmic, metaphysical, cosmic, and spiritual. Each chakra has been assigned its own color, but the colors used today are a modern attribution and crystals with much older chakra designations may not conform to this system.

Each chakra links to a specific area of life and to various organs and conditions. Loosely speaking, the chakras below the waist are primarily physical, although blockages can affect the functioning of the endocrine gland with resultant personality traits. Those in the upper torso are aligned to emotional functioning and the psyche, and blockages create psychosomatic conditions. Those in the head function on a mental and metaphysical intuitive/spiritual basis, but blockages can have physical repercussions. Imbalance, blockage, or disturbance in the chakras create dis-ease that ultimately manifests in your physical body, but which can be restored to equilibrium before physical illness results.

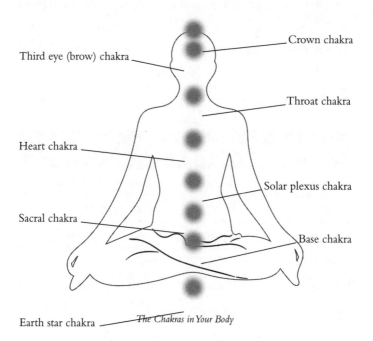

Crown chakra

Third eye (brow) chakra

Throat chakra

Heart chakra

Solar plexus chakra

Sacral chakra

Base chakra

Earth star chakra — *The Chakras in Your Body*

If a chakra is stuck open, it is known as a "blown" chakra and leads to negative conditions. A blown chakra is particularly vulnerable to outside influence, as there is no protection or filtering. Similarly, a chakra can be stuck in the closed position, leading to blockages and negative qualities manifesting. A chakra may be blocked because of your own past experiences or because other people "put a block" on it—that is, they control you or don't want you to sense what is really going on, and so on. Chakra imbalances can be rectified and the chakras can be harmonized to work together by placing crystals of the appropriate vibration over the chakras for 10 to 15 minutes.

Chakra	Color attribution	Function
Earth star	Brown	Grounding; protection
Base	Red	Energizing; survival
Sacral	Orange	Creating; activating
Solar plexus	Yellow	Nurturing; feeling
Heart	Green	Healing emotional distress; radiating love
Throat	Blue	Opening communication; expressing oneself
Brow (third eye)	Indigo	Metaphysical attunement
Crown	White/ purple	Opening intuition and higher awareness

Exercise: Opening the Earth Star

The earth star chakra is located about a foot (30cm) beneath and between your feet.

1. To open the earth star, picture a dinner plate-sized vortex of energy spinning beneath your feet as you stand barefoot with them slightly apart.

2. The earth star has a root that goes deep down into the center of the Earth. Picture two branches coming up from the Earth that join the soles of your feet.

3. Bounce a little as you make the connection to strengthen it. Feel how it grounds you and holds you safely in incarnation (gives you protection and connects your subtle energy and physical bodies together), channeling energy from the Earth to your feet.

Chakra Spin

Turn your hand with a crystal held firmly so that the point traces a spiral. Spiraling a crystal out from a chakra opens and cleanses it. Spiraling back in to a chakra re-energizes and seals it. Let your hand tell you the direction in which to move the crystal. Despite what you may read in books, individual chakras have their own direction of spin and reversing yours may not be appropriate, so allow your intuition or the crystal to guide you to do what is appropriate. Use a wand or a crystal with a point—its point should face outward for cleansing and face inward for recharging (you may need to cleanse the crystal in between).

Exercise:
Crystal Cleansing and Chakra Recharging

Having all your chakras open and functioning at an optimum level enhances your general well-being and helps you negotiate your way through changes in your life. This chakra cleansing can be done at any time. Use purified and activated crystals for the chakra recharging. If a chakra feels particularly "sticky"—if it sticks or "bumps" over the spot—spiral the crystal out, cleanse it, and then spiral it in again. You may like to ask a friend to assist with this next part, but if not have all your crystals close by so you can reach them easily when lying down.

1. Lie down and place Smoky Quartz (or another brown crystal) between and slightly below your feet. Picture

light and energy radiating out from the crystal into the earth star chakra for two or three minutes and be aware that the chakra is being cleansed and its spin regulated. The chakra then holds you anchored into incarnation and the vibration of Earth.

2. Place a red crystal on your base chakra. Picture light and energy radiating out from the crystal into the base chakra for a few moments.

3. Place an orange crystal on your sacral chakra, just below the navel. Feel the cleansing process.

4. Place a Citrine or another yellow crystal on your solar plexus chakra.

5. Place a green crystal on your heart chakra.

6. Place a blue crystal on your throat chakra.

7. Place an indigo crystal on your brow (third eye) chakra.

8. Place an Amethyst or another lilac/purple crystal on your crown.

9. Place a white crystal (point facing down, if it has one) above your head.

10. Now take your attention slowly from the soles of your feet up the midline of your body, feeling how each chakra has become balanced and harmonized.

11. Remain still and relaxed, breathing deep down into your belly and counting to seven before you exhale. As you breathe in and hold your breath, feel the energy of the crystals re-energizing the chakras and from there radiating out through your whole being.

12. When you feel ready, gather your crystals up, starting from above the crown. As you reach the earth star chakra, be aware of a grounding cord anchoring you to the earth from your physical body.

13. Cleanse your crystals thoroughly.

Closing the Chakras

Removing the crystal and placing your hand over the site closes a chakra down, as does placing a piece of Flint over the chakra. Note: Keeping your earth star chakra open helps to ground your energies unless you are in an area that has disturbed toxic Earth energies.

Useful Chakra Crystals

Below is a list of crystals and the chakras and functions they are best suited for:

- **Alignment:** Aurora Quartz (Anandalite™); Citrine; Graphic Smoky Quartz in Feldspar; Kyanite; Quantum Quattro; Quartz.

- **Alignment with physical body:** Amber; Graphic Smoky Quartz; Que Sera.

- **Balance (restoring):** Graphic Smoky Quartz; Sunstone.

- **Base chakra:** Bloodstone; Carnelian; Cuprite; Fire Agate; Garnet; Graphic Smoky Quartz; Pink Tourmaline; Red Calcite; Red Jasper; Smoky Quartz.

- **Blockages (dissolving):** Bloodstone; Clear Quartz; Graphic Smoky Quartz; Lapis Lazuli; Rainbow Mayanite.

- **Blown chakras (repairing):** Fire Agate; Graphic Smoky Quartz; Que Sera; Rainbow Mayanite.

- **Brow (third eye) chakra:** Apophyllite; Aquamarine; Azurite; Herkimer Diamond; Iolite; Kunzite; Lapis

Lazuli; Lepidolite; Malachite with Azurite; Moldavite; Preseli Bluestone; Purple Fluorite; Royal Sapphire; Sodalite; Yellow Labradorite.

- **Cleansing:** Amethyst; Bloodstone; Calcite; Citrine; Quartz; Gold and Silver Healer; Graphic Smoky Quartz; Que Sera; Rainbow Mayanite; Tourmaline wand.

- **Crown chakra:** Angelite; Beryl; Clear Tourmaline; Golden Lepidolite; Larimar; Moldavite; Petalite; Phenacite; Purple Jasper; Purple Sapphire; Quartz; Selenite.

- **Earth star chakra:** Boji Stone; Brown Jasper; Cuprite; Fire Agate; Flint; Graphic Smoky Quartz in Feldspar; Hematite; Mahogany Obsidian; Rhodonite; Smoky Elestial Quartz; Smoky Quartz; Tourmaline.

- **Energy leakage (preventing):** Ajoite with Shattuckite; Graphic Smoky Quartz; Green Aventurine; Labradorite; Quartz; Que Sera.

- **Heart chakra:** Aventurine; Chrysocolla; Danburite; Green Jasper; Green Quartz; Green Tourmaline; Jade; Jadeite; Kunzite; Morganite; Muscovite; Pink Tourmaline; Rhodochrosite; Rhodonite; Rose Quartz; Ruby; Variscite; Watermelon Tourmaline.

- **Protection:** Apache Tear; Graphic Smoky Quartz; Jet; Labradorite; Quartz.

- **Sacral/navel chakra:** Blue Jasper; Citrine; Orange Calcite; Orange Carnelian; Que Sera; Topaz.

- **Solar plexus chakra:** Citrine; Golden Beryl; Jasper; Malachite; Rhodochrosite; Tiger's Eye; Yellow Tourmaline.

- **Strengthening:** Graphic Smoky Quartz; Magnetite (Lodestone); Quartz; Que Sera.

- **Throat chakra:** Amber; Amethyst; Aquamarine; Blue Lace Agate; Kunzite; Lepidolite; Topaz; Tourmaline; Turquoise.

DAY 7

Crystals for Personal Protection

Today's Crystals

Basic: Black Tourmaline
Advanced: Tantalite

All around you there are unseen vibrations, imperceptible emanations, and subtle energy fields. You are surrounded by thoughts, feelings, imprints, and impressions that can subtly disturb your sense of well-being. A filter is needed. Energy protection helps you to screen yourself against this invisible invasion, and this is our topic for today.

Toxic energy is an intrusion that is silent, invisible, and yet very powerful in its draining effect. This unseen force operates not in the physical world, but at the psychic, mental and emotional levels of being. Psychic protection is subtle, creating an impermeable barrier around the aura— the biomagnetic energy field that surrounds you. Psychic protection acts as an interface with some else's energy field—invaluable if you work with other people, particularly those who are troubled or ill.

You need psychic protection if:

- You work closely with other people.

- People naturally gravitate to you with their troubles.

- You give a great deal of energy to other people.

- Certain people or places leave you feeling drained and tired.

- You are sensitive to atmospheres.

- You feel low if a friend is depressed or unhappy.

- You feel on edge if a friend is angry.

- You live with your head in the clouds.

- You are anxious, nervy, on edge all the time.

- You have invisible feelers out, testing the air around you.

- You feel perpetually tired, listless, or hopeless.

- You feel invaded, somehow *not yourself.*

- You dwell on things, turning them over and over in your mind.

- Someone shows particularly strong animosity to you.

- You are a water sign: Cancer, Scorpio, or Pisces.

- You are psychic or a healer.

But everyone benefits from personal energy protection!

Psychic Self-protection

The key to good protection is to find exactly the right crystal for the situations in which you find yourself. Crystals have been used for this purpose for thousands of years, as have crystal essences—subtle, vibrational energies that resonate with our aura to strengthen it and to cleanse the space around us (*see Day 11*). Black Tourmaline, Smoky Quartz, and Amethyst were traditionally used for protection, particularly for turning back ill-wishing or jealousy, and are highly protective when worn around the neck. Tantalite provides 21st-century protection—protection from technology, electromagnetic pollution, and from the pressures of modern society. A Labradorite crystal, with its unexpected scintillating flash of blue, is a wonderful energy protector that also pulls in spiritual power. An excellent crystal for healers and those who work with other people, it enhances intuition while creating an interface that prevents taking on other people's problems, or negative thoughts and energies.

Exercise:
Protecting Yourself

1. Wear a Black Tourmaline or a Labradorite crystal around your neck.

2. For advanced protection, either wear a Tantalite placed in a wire spiral, or use the power of your imagination to create a Tantalite "cage" around your whole body.

3. Whenever you feel the need for additional protection, mentally shout "Tantalite" and feel that protective cage strengthening around you.

Combating Energy Vampires

It is all too easy to lose energy to other people. The main symptoms are a feeling of weariness or slight depression, low energy, and a tugging or tweaking pain under your left armpit. This leaching occurs through the solar plexus, but happens to a greater extent through the spleen chakra or energy portal located about a hand's breadth beneath the left armpit. If you get a nagging pain there, an energy vampire is at work. This may be a family member, a partner or a friend, a client or a work colleague. Fortunately, the antidote is simple: Unhook them and close the energy portal.

The Spleen Chakra

The spleen chakra is the sphere of assertion and empowerment. If it is imbalanced, you are likely to have anger issues or suffer constant irritation, with your body turning in to attack itself. If the chakra is too open, other people can draw on your energy, leaving you energetically depleted, particularly at the immune level. Typical dis–eases that arise from depletion are lethargy, anaemia, and low blood sugar.

Exercise:
Closing the Energy Portal

1. Cleanse your spleen chakra by spiraling out a Flint, Quartz point, or Rainbow Mayanite stone to clear any hooks or energetic connections, or use a Jasper tie-cutter.

2. Tape a Green Aventurine, Green Fluorite, Jade, or Tantalite crystal over the spleen chakra, or wear one on a long chain so that it reaches down to the end of your breastbone.

TODAY'S CRYSTALS

Basic: Black Tourmaline
Vibration: Earthy

- Deflects negative energies.

- Protects against geo-pollutants, electro-magnetic frequency (EMF), and radiation.

- Turns back anger, ill-wishing, and attack.

- Increases physical vitality and strengthens the immune system.

  Tape this crystal to your mobile phone, put it next to your computer or other source of EMF, or keep it in your pocket. Place it between your house and a source of radiation or EMF.

Advanced: Tantalite
Vibration: High

- Soaks up negative energy and guards against psychic vampirism, ill-wishing, or environmental pollution.

- Blocks invasion by alien or adverse forces and creates an energetic grid around the body to "repel boarders."

- Removes hooks, attachments, implants, mental imperatives, and core beliefs lodged in the etheric or the physical bodies.

- Shields the body so that nothing else attaches.

- Stabilizes the environment.

- Revitalizes a sense of purpose and direction.

~

DAY 8

Combating Subtle Pollutants

Today's Crystal

Shungite

These days most of us are bombarded with unseen EMF radiation or geo-pollutants (adverse energy lines and toxicity in the ground) to which some of us can be adversely receptive, especially if we are psychic or energy-sensitive. We can feel drained and ill. Some people are affected in this way, others fortunately are not.

I live near an electricity sub-station—not my first choice of location, as I'm all too aware of the detrimental effects of EMF emissions on my energy field. I have, however, turned this around to heal and re-energize myself with the use of crystals. Firstly, I asserted that the emissions would help me to heal, transmuting negative energy and re-energizing me. On moving in I gridded (*see Day 13*) the garden with pieces of Black Tourmaline, positioning one at each corner and, for good measure, I put these around my bed as well. I placed Amazonite, Amethyst, Herkimer Diamonds, and Smoky Quartz points on the windowsills (with the points pointing away from the house to deflect the energy). Then Shungite came into my life and I added this into the mix, along with Que Sera. The house now feels energetically clear and, on dowsing, registers no adverse EMF emissions.

The crystals I used are equally effective for any "bad vibes" that may be affecting your home or workplace. They are excellent for combating "sick building syndrome." My computer is surrounded with Shungite, Fluorite, and Lepidolite to further protect my energy, but you could use Smoky Quartz or Amethyst for this. If you, like me, are sensitive to mobile phone emanations, then taping a piece of Shungite, Black Tourmaline, or Smoky Quartz onto the phone protects your auric field.

Exercise: Protecting Yourself Against EMFs

1. Switch on your computer or mobile phone or stand close to your television. With your hands sense the energy field around it and feel the effect it has on your body and your energy. If it has no effect, you need go no further. If there is an adverse response, place Shungite between you and the EMF source. Feel the energy change as the emissions are blocked.

2. Move the Shungite around your body to find the best place for it. You can wear it over your thymus (just above the heart), place it over the spleen chakra under your left arm, or wherever it feels it is working best.

Note: If you begin to feel tired when wearing or using Shungite, cleanse it immediately. It is sensible to have at least two pieces, one in use and one being cleansed.

Working with Shungite

Vibration: High

I'm devoting more space than usual to this incredible crystal although there is a Shungite entry in *101 Power*

Crystals, along with a photograph that palpates with its energy, there is little other information out there. Most of the research was done in Russia where it is used to cloak the EMF "signature" from ships and submarines, and also for healing purposes.

Shungite contains virtually all the minerals in the periodic table. Its phenomenal shielding power arises from its unique formation. A rare carbon mineral, it is composed of fullerenes: 'Buckyballs' (spherical) or 'Buckytubes' (cylindrical). Each tiny, hollow Buckyball has between 20 to 500 carbon atoms. Fullerenes empower nanotechnology, being excellent geothermal and electromagnetic conductors, and yet Shungite shields from EMF emissions.

Something of an enigma, Shungite is found only in Karelia, northern Russia and is at least 2 billion years old. It formed before organic life was established and yet carbon-based minerals normally arise from decayed organic matter, such as ancient forests. It has been suggested that an enormous meteorite hit the Earth and created the crater in which Lake Onega later formed. It is postulated that micro-organisms were swimming in a soupy-sea and that the seabed formed the Shungite deposit. What is known is that although the lake is highly polluted, water that has passed through the

Shungite bed has been purified, and is used down-river at the healing spa. This site has been used as a healing spa for hundreds of years.

Research has shown that Shungite is anti-viral and anti-bacterial. It absorbs that which is hazardous to health whether it be pesticides, free radicals, bacteria, and the like, or EMF, microwave, and other vibrational emissions. It transforms water into a biologically active, life-enhancing substance, while at the same time removing harmful micro-organisms and pollutants. Moreover, it boosts physical well-being and has a powerful effect on the immune system. Restoring emotional equilibrium, Shungite transmutes stress into a potent energetic recharge. A Shungite pyramid placed by the bed counteracts insomnia and headaches, and eliminates the physiological effects of stress. Wear Shungite or place it on the source of EMF emissions such as computers and cell phones to eliminate their detrimental effect on sensitive human energy systems.

It is important to note that as Shungite is a rapid absorber of negative energy and pollutants, it needs to be cleansed frequently.

Exercise: Making Shungite Water

1. Immerse about 0.35lb (10 grams) of Shungite in 34 fl oz (1 litre) of water for at least 48 hours to therapeutically activate the water. (I find it best to place the Shungite in a mesh bag in the bottom of a filter jug. I continuously top up the water as I use it and I cleanse the crystals frequently.)

2. Drink several glasses a day for maximum effect.

DAY 9

Crystals for Creating a Safe Space

Today's Crystals

Basic: Labradorite

Advanced: Graphic Smoky Quartz in Feldspar, also known as Zebra Stone

Many crystals have strong protective powers that we can harness. Today you are going to learn how to create your own safe space and keep your environment energetically clean.

Houses and other spaces have a subtle energetic history. An imprint is left by people who live there. Neighbors add their vibes, as do events that have previously occurred there.

Crystals counteract these emanations and put beneficial energies in their place.

A crystal has benefits that you feel rather than see. A protective crystal such as a Black Tourmaline, a Graphic Smoky Quartz or an Elestial Quartz placed outside the front door protects the whole house, preventing an influx of negative vibes. Similarly, a Carnelian in the same place invites in abundance and good vibes. If the crystal you are using has a point, point it away from your house to deflect negative energy and transmute it into positive. If you want your home to be filled with love and harmony, placing a Rose Quartz crystal just inside the front door does the trick.

How do you find the right spot in which to place your stone? The crystal will probably tell you! But you can also dowse for it (*see Day 1*). Some places are obvious. For example, a large piece of Rose Quartz placed by your bed encourages love and harmony. The same crystal put near the wall you share with noisy neighbors radiates out vibrations to calm them down. Remember to clean the crystal regularly.

Exercise: Living or Working in a Safe Space

1. To keep a room energetically clean, place a large piece of Black Tourmaline, Calcite, Graphic Smoky Quartz, Smoky Quartz, or Tourmalinated Quartz in a position where it won't be disturbed and ask it to transmute negative energies. Remember to cleanse it frequently.

2. You can also make a crystal essence to spritz around the space (*see Day 11*).

Ghosties, Wee Beasties, and Things That Go Bump in the Night!

If you are troubled by restless spirits, gremlins, or the impact of events that occurred in the past, a crystal is of great assistance. Quite apart from their own cleansing properties, crystals make great carriers for safe-space and clearing essences, and I find the synergistic effect much stronger than using an essence or a crystal alone. To deal with ghosts I put a few drops of Petaltone Astral Clear on a clear Quartz crystal, ask it to send the spirit to the light, and leave it overnight to do its work. For slightly more troublesome spirits, Petaltone Special 8 works well, particularly when you use Quartz or Labradorite as a carrier. To keep a space energetically purified and filled with spiritual light for long periods I put Petaltone Z14 on a large piece of Selenite—it works for six months and more.

Useful Crystals for Creating a Safe Space

Below is a list of actions that are necessary for creating a safe place and the crystals that you can use for them:

- **Absorbing geopathic stress:** Black Tourmaline; Smoky Quartz; Tantalite.

- **Cleansing negative energies:** Amber; Bloodstone; Shungite.

- **Clearing environmental pollution:** Graphic Smoky Quartz in Feldspar; Malachite (particularly good for radioactive emissions); Turquoise.

- **Deflecting psychic attacks:** Black Tourmaline; Shungite; Tantalite.

- **Neutralizing EMFs:** Amazonite; Black Tourmaline; Fluorite; Smoky Quartz.

- **Replacing negative vibrations with positive, loving vibes:** Amethyst; Rose Quartz; Selenite.

Gridding

We'll be looking at grids in more detail on Days 13 and 20, but as they play an important part in space-clearing and maintaining a safe space, we'll have a brief look at them now. Gridding is the art of placing crystals to create an energetic net to protect and energize space. The easiest way to grid a room or another space is to place a crystal in each corner, as this creates an energy grid across the whole room. However, you can grid the room with whatever pattern feels right at the time. Dowsing establishes the exact placement for crystals when gridding. Join the crystals with a wand or a long-point crystal by imagining you are drawing a line to link them, using a Quartz or a Lemurian to set the grid.

When gridding, the lines of force may have to pass through walls and solid objects. Use the power of your mind or a crystal wand to connect the points by taking it up to the wall, seeing it pass through the wall, and then walking around to the other side to recommence the line.

Exercise: Creating a Safe-space Grid

1. Place small pieces of Graphic Smoky Quartz or Black Tourmaline in each corner your house or a particular room to keep out bad vibes. Use ethereal white Selenite, or raw or polished Labradorite to draw in spiritual light to assist in your work or your daily and spiritual life.

2. Join the stones up with the power of your mind or a Quartz wand to create a three-dimensional energetic grid that protects your entire space.

TODAY'S CRYSTALS

Basic: Labradorite
Vibration: High

♦ Protective, so deflects negative energies.

♦ Prevents energy leakage and creates an energetic interface so that you are aware of other people's feelings or of environmental energies but do not take them on.

- Raises consciousness and the Earth's spiritual energies on the planet.

- Accesses spiritual purpose.

- Aligns intellect and intuition.

- Relieves stress, regulates metabolism—wear around neck over the thymus gland in the center of the upper chest.

~

Advanced: Graphic Smoky Quartz in Feldspar (Zebra Stone)
Vibration: High

- A fairly new discovery from Madagascar (available from the US as Zebra Stone).

- Strongly purifying and grounding, and helps you feel safe in physical incarnation.

- Invigorating for the body, it infuses dynamic energy and a feeling of well-being.

- Assists in making you feel safe in traumatic situations, getting to the core and instilling trust.

- Opens and cleanses all the chakras and activates metaphysical abilities—plus is excellent for strengthening the structures of the physical or subtle bodies.

- A shamanic stone that enables traveling silently through the lower realms, it imparts the stealth of a big cat.

- Insists on integrity in its use, helping you to find a creative way to approach your goals.

~

DAY 10

Crystals for Energy Enhancement

Today's Crystals

Basic: Carnelian

Advanced: Que Sera (Vulcanite)

All crystals vibrate with energy, but they resonate at different frequencies and in different patterns according to their mineral make-up. Today we are taking a closer look at crystals that give you an instant energy boost.

The key to energy enhancement is to surround yourself with good vibrations and to be positive. While fear attracts the very things you are afraid of and erodes your energy, joy enhances it. An upbeat outlook attracts experiences to support and energize you. If you are joyful and feel that life is abundant and nourishing, life flows well and good things come to you.

Here's a useful checklist of things you can do:

1. Be in a space that feels good—if it doesn't, change it (*see Day 9*).

2. Think positive thoughts and have positive expectations (avoid fear).

3. Do the things you enjoy.

4. Be with people who boost your energy.

5. Wear appropriate crystals or grid them around you (*see Days 13 and 20*).

Exercise: Bringing in Good Vibes

For this exercise you need: Quartz, Que Sera or Selenite.

This crystal visualization combines the power of your mind with that of your crystals. Visualization is seeing things in your mind's eye. Closing your eyes and looking up to the point between and slightly above the center of your eyebrows helps images to form, as does letting your eyes go out of focus when looking into a crystal. However, you don't need to *see* anything to *feel* the benefit. (You may like to record this visualization or have a friend read it out to you.)

1. Sit comfortably and close your eyes. Look up to the point between and above your eyebrows.

2. Open your palm chakras to radiate the crystal energy.

3. Hold your crystal in whichever hand feels most comfortable.

4. Breathe gently. Let your attention go to the top of your head, taking the hand with the crystal there. Hold the crystal as far as you can reach above your head.

5. Imagine that someone has switched on a very bright white light above your head and this is focused through your crystal. Feel the brightness and the warmth of this light mingling with the vibrant crystal energies. It is full of good vibrations. Feel the crystal light begin to move down through your head (move your crystal downward as you go). As it moves the crystal light seeks out any dark places, filling it with light and joy.

6. The crystal light moves through your skull, penetrating all the folds and creases of your brain, filling it. The

vibrations feel potent and tingly; your mind opens up and accepts the happiness in the crystal light, which expands into your whole head. Your eyes are bright, your hearing acute. Your nose and mouth fill with the crystal light as you breathe in bubbles of crystal energy.

7. Next, the crystal light passes on down through your throat and neck and into your shoulders, arms, and hands. You feel the vibrations tingling down to your fingertips. The bubbles of crystal light pass into your lungs, energizing as they go. Your back has a column of crystal light supporting it and ribs of crystal light around it, as the crystal light moves on down through your internal organs, illuminating them as it goes.

8. Now be aware of the crystal light entering your heart, dissolving any pain or grief stored there, filling your heart with joy and good vibrations. Feel your blood picking up the vibrations as it passes through your heart and lungs. It helps to carry the crystal light to every part of your body.

9. When the crystal light reaches your solar plexus, it pauses awhile. As you breathe, the crystal light cleanses the emotions that you hold in your solar plexus, encouraging the joyous ones and transmuting any painful feelings.

10. Then the crystal light moves on down into your hips and belly. When it reaches the base of your spine and your

reproductive organs, you feel your creative energy begin to resonate in harmony with the vibration of the crystal light. Let this creative force flow wherever it will.

11. Allow the crystal light to move on down through your thighs and legs to your feet until your toes tingle.

12. Be aware that your whole body is filled with this vibrating crystal light. Your energy is replenished. Your body is in balance, your emotions are harmonious, your thoughts positive.

13. Curl the energy down into the *dantien* (an energy center in traditional Chinese medicine) that is situated just below your navel. Store the energy here until you need it. A deep breath or holding the crystal over this place is all that is needed to release the energy when required.

14. This action "switches off" the crystal light, but you remain filled with it.

15. Take your attention down to your feet. Be very aware of the contact they make with the earth. Feel them holding you and grounding you on the earth and into your body. Then, when you are ready, open your eyes.

Today's Crystals

Basic: Carnelian
Vibration: Earthy

- A powerfully energizing crystal.

- Grounds and anchors you into your present surroundings.

- Protects against rage and resentment.

- Increases fertility and creativity.

- Motivates success in business and brings abundance.

- Continually charges-up your energy—keep one in your car to protect against road rage or place one inside your front door to draw in abundance.

~

Advanced: Que Sera (Vulcanite)
Vibration: High

- A potent, synergistic combination of Calcite, Clinozoisite, Feldspar, Iron, Kaolinite, Leucozone, Magnetite, and Quartz.

- An excellent all-round healer and power source containing high-vibration bioscalar waves (*see Day 11*) and abundant Qi (life force).

- Cleanses and re-energizes all the chakras.

- An excellent shield against Wi-Fi emanations and other EMF pollutants.

- Recharges and balances the meridians and organs of the subtle and physical bodies.

- Activates neurotransmitters to optimize the energetic circuit.

- Helps you find constructive solutions and confidence about your actions—with this crystal you co-create your own future.

~

DAY 11

Healing
with Crystals

Today's Crystals

Basic: Bloodstone
Advanced: Quantum Quattro

For millennia one of the primary uses of crystals has been for healing. This is our topic for today.

Crystals bring about healing holistically by balancing mind, body, and spirit. They focus and direct energy to a specific point on the body or to an emotional or mental blockage. Dis-ease is gently dissolved; imbalances are corrected. Crystals also assist by helping you to drop into a theta brainwave state. Theta waves induce a deep state of relaxation in which your subconscious mind and your psychic immune system can be accessed. All illnesses ultimately stem from a state of dis-ease (physical imbalances, blocked feelings, suppressed emotions, and negative thinking which, if not reversed, lead to illness). A theta wave state helps your body return to equilibrium and so can be utilized for profound healing, particularly as it interacts with the bioscalar waves (*see page 81*) naturally created by crystals.

In healing, crystals can be placed over the chakras (*see Days 6, 12, 14, and 15*), directly over organs, or laid out around the body to create a healing grid (*see Day 13*). If your crystal has a point, placing it with the point facing outward draws negative energy away from the body, while putting it with the point facing inward draws energy into the body. You can do a complete chakra cleanse and recharge (*see Day 6*) if you wish, or you can just cleanse a specific chakra if you identify with an issue associated with that chakra. For example, throat or lung conditions respond to well if you treat the throat chakra and you can lessen abdominal distress by treating the base or sacral chakras. We will look further into this in the days that follow.

Bioscalar Waves

To my mind bioscalar waves are one of the most exciting discoveries in healing. A bioscalar wave is a standing energy field created when two fields interact from different angles and counteract each other so that the field reverts to a static "state of potentiality." Many of the new crystals, such as Aurora Quartz (Anandalite™) or Rainbow Quartz, Que Sera, Quantum Quattro, and Rainbow Mayanite contain concentrated bioscalar energy. All healing crystals probably have this energy within their matrix, generating it through their crystalline structure. Research suggests that bioscalar waves assist cell membranes in switching on the most beneficial genetic function and switching off detrimental patterns encoded within DNA. It has been demonstrated that bioscalar waves directly influence tissue at a microscopic level, bringing about a healing balance. They have been shown to enhance the immune and endocrine systems, stabilize chemical processes, improve the coherence of the biomagnetic field, and accelerate healing at all levels. At a subtle level, they release stored emotions and ingrained thoughts from the cellular structures of the body, removing a root cause of psychosomatic dis-ease.

The Immune System

Your immune system is what keeps you healthy, fighting off bacteria and viruses. In addition to the physical immune system, you also have a subtle, psychic one that interacts with crystal energy. When this is stimulated, well-being ensues. One of the major governing points of the immune system is the thymus gland, which is situated in the middle of your upper chest, about a hand's breadth below your throat.

Exercise: Stimulate Your Immunity

While Bloodstone has long been used to stimulate the immune system, Quantum Quattro is a much more recent discovery that heals through the synergy of several minerals. Both are effective immune stimulators.

1. Taking a cleansed and dedicated Bloodstone or Quantum Quattro, tap gently over your thymus gland in the center of your upper chest (either side of your breastbone may be more comfortable) for five minutes.

2. Alternatively, tape the stone in place and leave it there for several hours.

Crystal Essences

Crystal essences are a gentle way to use the healing properties of stones, as the vibrations are transferred to water. Use only cleansed, non-toxic crystals or the indirect method (*see below*). Essences can be taken as drops, or spritzed (sprayed) or rubbed on the skin.

1. Place a crystal in spring water in a glass or crystal bowl (or, for the indirect method, place the crystal in a small glass bowl and then place this in the water so that there is no direct contact between the crystal and the water).

2. Place the bowl in the sun for several hours or overnight in moonlight as appropriate.

3. Remove the crystal and add the activated water to one-third as much again of brandy, vodka, or white rum to preserve it. Bottle, label, and store in a cool place. This is the mother tincture.

4. To make a dosage bottle, add seven drops of the mother tincture to a small dropper bottle filled with one third brandy, vodka, or white rum to two-thirds spring water. Or fill a small spray bottle with spring water and add seven drops of tincture.

5. Take seven drops three times a day, rub it onto the inside of one of your wrists, over the site of dis-ease or the corresponding chakra, or spritz it around your aura or your environment.

Crystal First-aid Kit

Amethyst

Cleansing; protecting; stabilizing; tranquilizing; transmuting; opening

- *Organs*: Lungs; intestines; brain
- *Gland*: Pineal
- *Systems*: Endocrine; digestive; metabolic; nervous; immune; skeletal; digestive; subtle bodies
- *Chakras*: Brow (third eye); throat; crown

Bloodstone

Cleansing; protecting; revitalizing; stimulating

- *Organs*: Liver; intestines; kidneys; spleen; bladder
- *Gland*: Thymus
- *Systems*: Immune; circulation; lymphatic; metabolic
- *Chakras*: Heart; base

Blue Lace Agate

Cooling; calming; opening; activating

- *Organs*: Pancreas; brain; throat
- *Glands*: Thyroid; parathyroid
- *Systems*: Lymphatic; skeletal; nervous
- *Chakra*: Throat

Carnelian

Energizing; stimulating; cleansing; stabilizing; grounding

- *Organs*: Reproductive; kidneys; intestines
- *Gland*: Adrenals
- *Systems*: Metabolic; reproductive
- *Chakras*: Base; sacral; spleen

Clear Quartz

Energizing; absorbing; storing; purifying; balancing; releasing; and regulating energy

- *Organs*: All
- *Glands*: Pituitary; pineal
- *Systems*: Immune; aura
- *Chakras*: All

Green Aventurine

Cleansing; activating; regulating; stabilizing

- *Organs*: Heart; adrenals; lungs; sinuses; eyes
- *Gland*: Thymus
- *Systems*: Mental; nervous; muscular; urogenital; connective tissue
- *Chakras*: Heart; spleen

Rose Quartz

Sedating; releasing; assimilating; forgiving; restoring

- *Organs*: Heart; lungs; kidneys; genitals; liver
- *Glands*: Thymus; adrenals
- *Systems*: Circulatory; lymphatic
- *Chakra*: Heart

Smoky Quartz

Cleansing; protecting; grounding; pain-relieving

- *Organs*: Heart; muscles; nerves; back
- *Gland*: None
- *Systems*: Reproductive; nervous
- *Chakras*: Earth star; base

Sodalite

Regulating fluids; cooling; stabilizing; releasing

- *Organs:* Vocal cords; larynx
- *Glands:* Pineal; thyroid
- *Systems:* Lymphatic; immune; metabolic
- *Chakras:* Throat; brow (third eye)

See also Que Sera (Day 10), Quantum Quattro (Day 11), and Golden Healer (Day 12).

TODAY'S CRYSTALS

Basic: Bloodstone

Vibration: Earthy

- One of the oldest healing stones used by humanity (its documented use goes back over 5,000 years).

- Associated with the blood and the kidneys.

- Purifies lymph, detoxifies the liver, improves circulation, strengthens the immune system, and stimulates production of T-cells.

- Sedates when systems are overactive; stimulates when they are underactive.

- Reduces mental confusion and imparts alertness.

- Relieves chronic conditions.

~

Advanced:
Quantum Quattro
Vibration: High

- A master healer and a strong mental cleanser.

- A combination of Chrysocolla on Smoky Quartz, Dioptase, Malachite, and Shattuckite.

- Brings the body back into balance and when placed on an area of imbalance, whether environmental or physical, it restores equilibrium.

- Has a dramatic effect on the human energy field, strengthening the immune system and DNA.

- Protective and absorbs toxic energies.

- Clears psychic attacks.

- Can balance mind, body, and emotions if one crystal is placed on the third eye and another on the solar plexus chakra.

- Heals the effects of grief; draws out deep feelings and psychosomatic causes; breaks unwanted ties and outworn patterns.

- Supports a positive attitude to life.

~

DAY 12

Crystals for Physical Healing

Today's Crystals

Basic: Jasper

Advanced: Gold Healer

Today we will delve deeper into using crystals for physical healing. It can be argued that physical illness starts in one of four ways:

1. Through the invasion of pathogens such as bacteria or viruses.

2. Through a disturbance in the organs, cells, or DNA.

3. Through the psychosomatic effect of the mind and the emotions (*see Days 14 and 15*).

4. Direct injury to the body.

Personally, I perceive dis-ease (as opposed to injury) as starting in what I call the etheric blueprint: A subtle energy grid that interpenetrates the physical body. To my eyes it carries not only present life dis-ease and emotional imprints, but also past-life attitudes and wounds that affect how the present-life physical body manifests and functions. That is to say, the dis-ease moves from the subtle to the physical. (There isn't room to go into this in depth here but see my work *The Book of Why* for further details).

Crystal healers believe that invasion or disturbance happens when the subtle energetic bodies that surround the physical, or the chakras that mediate the flow of life-force energy, are weakened or damaged, leaving the physical immune system depleted. The chakras, the linkage points between the different bodies, including the etheric blueprint, mediate the endocrine system. They have specific links to organs and bodily systems and "dis-ease" can be addressed by bringing the chakras and the subtle bodies into equilibrium, which then passes into the physical body. However, crystal energies also work directly on the site of pain, disturbance, or dis-ease.

The Chakras and Physiology

Below is a breakdown of the organs and body parts governed by the major chakras.

- **Base:** Gonads; adrenals; veins; lower back; rectum; lower extremities; lymph system; skeletal system (teeth and bones); immune system; prostate gland; kidneys; bladder and elimination system; sense of smell.

- **Sacral:** Testes; ovaries; uterus; lumbar and pelvic region; spleen; large intestine; immune system; kidneys; gallbladder; bladder and elimination system; sense of taste.

- **Solar plexus:** Pancreas; adrenals; stomach; liver; small intestine; digestive system; metabolism; lymphatic system; skin; sense of sight.

- **Heart:** Thymus; heart; circulation; lungs; shoulders; chest; sense of touch.

- **Throat:** Thyroid; throat; tonsils; nose; sinuses; tongue; ears; respiratory system; nervous system; skin; speech and body language.

- **Third eye:** Pineal gland; brain; neurological system; sinuses; eyes; ears; scalp; sense of hearing.

- **Crown:** Pituitary, hypothalamus; brain; spine; central nervous system; hair.

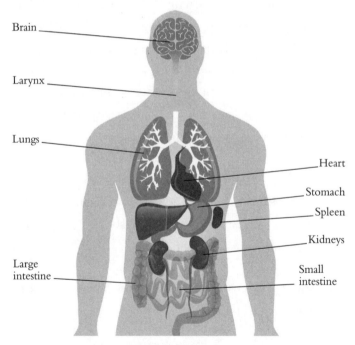

The Human Anatomy

Healing through the Chakras

Blockages or imbalances in the chakras create dis-ease on a physical, emotional, mental, or spiritual level, which can be treated by placing the appropriate crystals on the chakra in question. Chakras may be "blown," (stuck open) or closed; they may be over-active or inactive. The right crystal redresses the imbalance and brings the chakra back into equilibrium. Dowsing (*see Day 1*), or sensing the chakras with your palms, pinpoints which chakras need balancing, but you can also use a crystal such as a Lemurian or an Indicolite (Blue) Tourmaline, which "jumps," twitches, or tingles at a site of imbalance.

A chakra that is closed feels energy-less, lifeless. One that is too open or blown feels "buzzy" and "whizzy," with energy flying off in all directions, whereas a balanced chakra has a calm, centered energy with a measured spin. Some people state that chakras spin in a set direction, but I have found that people differ in this, so it's a question of discovering your own direction (a pendulum quickly shows you what this is). Each chakra functions holistically but today we'll focus on the three "lower" chakras, plus the past-life chakra:

Earth Star Chakra

Location: Beneath your feet

This chakra is the sphere of everyday reality and groundedness. Imbalances or blockages here lead to discomfort in your physical body, feelings of helplessness, and an inability to function practically in the world. Earth chakra imbalances pick up adverse environmental factors such as geopathic stress and toxic pollutants; when properly functioning, this chakra will filter these out. Typical dis-eases are lethargic in nature and include ME, arthritis, cancer, muscular disorders, depression, psychiatric disturbances, and auto-immune diseases.

Base Chakra

Location: Base of your spine/perineum

The base chakra is the sphere of basic survival instincts and security issues. Imbalances here lead to sexual disturbances and feelings of being stuck, anger, impotence, frustration, and an inability to let go. It also governs the "fight-or-flight" response. Typical dis-eases are constantly low-level in nature or flare up suddenly. They include stiffness in the joints; chronic lower back pain; renal, reproductive or rectal disorders (such as fluid retention or constipation, or, if the chakra is blown, diarrhea); varicose veins or hernias; the extremes of bipolar disorder; glandular disturbances; personality and anxiety disorders; and auto-immune diseases.

Sacral (Navel) Chakra

Location: Halfway between your belly button and the base of your pubic bone

The sacral chakra is the sphere of creativity, fertility, and acceptance of yourself as a powerful and sexual being. Imbalances lead to infertility and blocked creativity. This chakra is where "hooks" from other people may make themselves felt, particularly from sexual encounters. Typical dis-eases are toxic and psychosomatic, and include PMT and muscle cramps, reproductive blockages or diseases, impotence, infertility, allergies, addictions, eating disorders, diabetes, liver or intestinal dysfunction (for example, irritable bowel syndrome), chronic back pain, and urinary infections.

Past-life Chakras

Location: Behind the ears; along the bony ridge of the skull

The past-life chakras are the sphere of wisdom, skills, and instinctive knowing, though they also encompass emotional baggage and unfinished business. If these chakras are blown, you can be subconsciously overwhelmed by past-life trauma. Typical diseases are symbolic and metaphoric, reflecting old wounds and attitudes. These include reproductive difficulties, chronic pain or functional dis-ease, endocrine imbalances, and allergies and sensitivities.

Exercise:
Sensing Chakra Blockages

Choose a variety of crystals appropriate for this exercise (*see Days 1 and 6*). You could work on this exercise with a friend, checking out each other's chakras.

1. Open your palm chakras. Sit in an upright chair to begin with. If you are using your palm to check out the chakra, hold it, palm toward the chakra, about a hand's breadth out from your body. If you are dowsing to check the chakras, hold the pendulum level with the chakra—but use your palm to sense the energy first.

2. Begin with the earth star beneath your feet–you need to hold the pendulum or your palm just above your feet.

3. Sense the energy. Is it lifeless, or "buzzy," spinning, whirling off? Does it need stimulating or sedating? (Let your intuition help you to know the answer to this.)

4. Place different crystals between your feet in turn and note the changes in energy.

5. When you find the right crystal to balance the chakra, leave it in place and move on to the base chakra. Repeat for the base and sacral chakras. (Tape the crystals in place if appropriate or lie down.)

6. Check the past-life chakras behind your ears. Place appropriate crystals (this is easier if you are lying down).

7. When the three chakras are balanced and in equilibrium, remove the stones.

TODAY'S CRYSTALS

Basic: Jasper

(Earthy to high vibration depending on type)

- Comes in a whole range of colors and types and is excellent for revitalizing and stabilizing energy, making it perfect for physical healing. (Bloodstone is a Jasper).

- Sustains and supports during stressful times, bringing tranquility and wholeness.

- Aligns and energizes the chakras.

- Protects and grounds energy into the body, but does not overstimulate.

- Clears electromagnetic and environmental pollution.

~

Advanced: Gold Healer

(Exceedingly high vibration)

- A master multi-purpose, multi-dimensional healer for all conditions and intercellular levels.

- Restores the whole system holistically to optimum functioning.

- Amps up power exponentially and creating a multi-dimensional energy grid through its iron oxide content.

- Contains high concentrations of Qi and bioscalar waves.

- Purifies, aligns, and re-energizes the chakras, and rapidly releases outworn emotional or mental conditioning and inappropriate ties.

- A catalyst for profound spiritual health.

~

DAY 13

Grids for Health and Well-being

Today's Crystals

Crystals from your collection or from the grid suggestions

Today we are going to explore one of the most useful crystal healing techniques—gridding.

So what exactly is gridding? It's the art of placing stones in a layout or pattern on or around the body to create an energetic net to purify, heal, and energize. Grids are a great way to enfold yourself within crystal energies and harness their power. They encourage relaxation and induce a sense of well-being as they rebalance your subtle energies and re-energize your body.

In the following grids, the crystals are placed around your body—so you may like to enlist the assistance of a friend, although you can lay out your own grids. Remember to join the crystals with a wand or a long, pointed crystal to set the grid or, if you are working alone, you can use the power of your mind.

Six-pointed Star Grid

Six-pointed Star Grid

The six-pointed star grid is a traditional protection layout but it also creates a perfect cleansing and re-energizing grid. (You may like to ask a friend to help you lay out this grid around you.)

You need: Six cleansed and activated crystals (three, such as Smoky Quartz, for detoxing and three, such as Clear Quartz, for invigorating), and a crystal wand.

1. Lie down comfortably.

2. Place a Smoky Quartz or other detoxifying crystal below your feet, with the point, if it has one, facing down.

3. Spread your arms out and place a Smoky Quartz or other detoxifying crystal at the end of your fingertips, with the points, if they have them, facing out.

4. Join up the triangle with a wand or your mind, and lie in it for five minutes. As you breathe out, feel any tension, stress, or toxicity draining away from your body and being absorbed and transmuted by the crystals.

5. Place a Clear Quartz or other invigorating crystal above your head, with the point, if it has one, facing down.

6. Place two more crystals just below your knees (with their points facing in), level with the crystals at your fingertips.

7. Join up the triangle with a wand or your mind and lie in the six-pointed star for up to 15 minutes. Feel

purifying and invigorating white healing light coming in through the crystal above your head and filling your whole body.

8. When you are ready, collect up the invigorating and then the detoxifying crystals.

9. Stand up and connect to the earth beneath your feet, using your earth star chakra to ground you.

Five-pointed Star

Five-pointed Star Grid

The five-pointed star is a useful protection layout, but it also calls in universal love and healing to enhance your energy. If your crystals have points, lay them pointing toward the next crystal in the layout to channel the energy.

You need: Five cleansed and activated energizing stones (Quartz and Selenite are particularly useful for bringing in spiritual light), and a crystal wand.

1. Lie down comfortably with your legs and arms stretched out sideways so that your body forms a five-pointed star.

2. Lay a crystal above your head (if it has a point, face it toward your left foot).

3. Lay a crystal below your left foot (if it has a point, face it toward your right hand).

4. Lay a crystal at the end of your right hand (if it has a point face it toward your left hand).

5. Lay a crystal at the end of your left hand (if it has a point face it toward your right foot).

6. Lay a crystal below your right foot (if it has a point, face it toward your head).

7. Using a crystal wand or the power of your mind and starting with the crystal above your head, join the crystals to form the star, remembering to complete the circuit from your right foot to your head at the end.

8. Lie in the star for up to 15 minutes. Breathe gently and absorb the crystals' energies.

9. When you are ready, pick up the crystals in the reverse order to that in which you laid them out.

10. Stand up and make contact with the earth through the earth chakra beneath your feet.

Triangulation

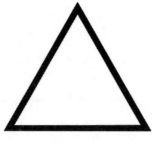

Triangulation

Triangulation neutralizes negative energy and brings in positive energy. It also provides protection or healing while you sleep, so this is a useful grid to build around your bed or to create a safe space.

You need: *Three cleansed and activated crystals, and a crystal wand*

1. Place a crystal (point facing down) above your head or at the head of your bed.

2. Place a crystal below your left leg (stretched out sideways) or at the left-hand corner of your bed.

3. Place a crystal below your right leg (stretched out sideways) or at the right-hand corner of your bed.

4. Bring your legs together, join up the triangle, and lie comfortably in the triangle for 15 minutes or during the night.

Figure of Eight

Figure of Eight Grid

Drawing spiritual energy down into the body, the figure of eight melds high-vibration energy with Earth energy drawn up from the feet to create a perfect balance. It is useful if you have been expanding your consciousness, as it anchors the energy into the physical body. It opens a cosmic anchor to ground you between the center of the Earth and the galactic center, creating core energy solidity that enables you to ride out energetic changes and channels high-vibration energy through your body and down to the Earth.

You need: Five cleansed and activated high-vibration stones, and five cleansed and activated grounding stones.

1. Lie down comfortably where you will not be disturbed for 15 minutes.

2. Starting on your left-hand side at your waist, place five high-vibration stones, equally spaced between the waist and the crown, up to your crown and down the other side.

3. Starting this time on your right-hand side, place five grounding stones below your waist down to your feet and up the other side. (You can sit up to do this and then lie back down again.)

4. Join up the stones with a wand or your mind. Remember to complete the circuit back to the first stone you placed.

Exercise: Lay Out a Grid

1. Choose the grid shape that most appeals to you from those shown above and select the most appropriate crystals (*see Day 1*).

2. Lay out the grid and lie in it. Notice how your energy changes. You may feel more peaceful and relaxed; uplifted and spiritually connected, or as though you are becoming more invigorated and energetic, or you may experience a wave of energy flowing through you. You may become hot or cold, shivery or fizzy.

3. If appropriate, try different crystals to feel the energizing, uplifting, or calming effect.

Useful Grid Crystals

- **Grounding and detoxifying crystals:** Black Tourmaline; Boji Stones; Bronzite; Mahogany Obsidian; Orange River Quartz; Smoky Elestial Quartz; Smoky Quartz; Tantalite.

- **High-vibration crystals:** Ocean Jasper; Petalite; Selenite; and high-vibration quartzes such as Amethyst; Azeztulite; Gold Healer; Mayanite; Nirvana; Rainbow Quartz; Satyaloka; Satyamani.

- **Re-energizing crystals:** Carnelian; Citrine; Golden Healer; Quantum Quattro; Que Sera; Red Jasper; Trummer Jasper.

DAY 14

Crystals for Emotional and Psychosomatic Healing

Today's Crystals

Basic: Rose Quartz
Advanced: Larimar

We all carry emotional baggage from the past: Disappointments, losses, and hurts—but some people are better at releasing this than others. Today our topic is how crystals can help us to heal emotionally and release psychosomatic illness.

Holding on to emotional baggage makes it difficult to adjust to life changes and it can create psychosomatic dis-ease, in which the "illness" reflects the cause—for example, heartbreak leads to heart attacks, rigidity to hardened arteries or joints, and so on. The cause lies deep in the subconscious mind, but psychosomatic illness is not simply "imagination," it presents underlying dis-ease in a symbolic fashion. Crystals gently dissolve baggage such as unresolved grief, heartbreak, jealousy, anger, and so on—even when these carry over from a previous life.

Negative Emotions and the Chakras

Negative emotions are held in the chakras and the subtle emotional body, and these have a profound effect on your well-being. Placing crystals on the appropriate chakra(s) for five to 15 minutes transmutes negative emotions into positive ones and enhances your capacity for joy. (As the negative emotion can be deeply ingrained, the crystals can be taped in place or the exercise repeated at least once daily for a week or more.)

Chakras for the Emotions

Solar Plexus Chakra

Location: Slightly above your waist

This chakra is the sphere of emotional communication and assimilation. Blockages lead to taking on other people's feelings and problems or to being overwhelmed by your own emotions. It affects the assimilation and utilization of energy, and concentration. Emotional "hooks" from other people can be found here. "Illness as theatre" occurs, playing out the emotional story through physical dis-ease. Its negative qualities are inferiority and clinginess, while its positive quality is emotional stability. Typical dis-eases are emotional and demanding, and include stomach ulcers, ME, "fight-or-flight" epinephrine (adrenaline) imbalances, insomnia, chronic anxiety, digestive problems, gallstones, pancreatic failure, eczema and other skin conditions, eating disorders, and phobias.

Heart Chakra

Location: Over your heart

The heart chakra is the sphere of love and nurturing. If your heart chakra is blocked, love cannot flourish, feelings such as jealousy are common, and there is enormous resistance to change. Its negative quality is possessiveness, while its positive qualities are compassion and peaceful harmony. Typical dis-eases are psychosomatic and reactive—for example, heart attacks, angina, chest infections, asthma, frozen shoulder, and ulcers.

Past-life Chakras (*see Day 12*)

Location: Behind the ears; along the bony ridge of the skull

As we saw on Day 12, the past-life chakras are the sphere of wisdom, skills, and instinctive knowing, but they also encompass emotional baggage and unfinished business. If the chakras are blown, you can be subconsciously overwhelmed by past-life trauma. Typical dis-eases are symbolic and metaphoric, reflecting past-life conditions or attitudes, or can be a direct carry-over, a karmic imprint, or a repetition.

There are negative and positive qualities associated with the chakras.

Chakra	Negative quality	Positive quality
Earth	Powerlessness	Empowerment
Base	Insecurity	Security
Sacral	Low self-esteem	Self-confidence
Solar Plexus	Inferiority	Empathy
Heart	Jealousy/ neediness	Compassion/ unconditional love
Brow (third eye)	Self-delusion	Emotional clarity
Past Life	Possessiveness/ fear	Openness/trust
Crown	Arrogance	Joy

Exercise:
Emotional Cleansing

Choose a crystal that feels right to you and ask it to clear any issues whether you consciously recognize them or not. You will also need a Smoky Quartz, preferably one with a point, and a crystal of unconditional love, such as Danburite, Rose Quartz, or Selenite.

1. Lie comfortably where you will not be disturbed.

2. Place a Smoky Quartz (point, if it has one, facing down) at your feet to absorb and transmute the emotional baggage you release.

3. Place your selected crystal over your solar plexus or other relevant chakra and ask that it dissolves your emotional baggage and that the Smoky Quartz absorbs the remnants. Consciously push the energy you release down your body and out of your feet into the Smoky Quartz for transmutation.

4. If you feel an unexplained ache, tugging, or pain anywhere in your body, place a crystal over it and ask that it be released and transmuted. Your intuition may give you a glimpse into the underlying causes but, if not, just let it dissolve without needing to know why it arose.

5. Place Danburite, Rose Quartz, Selenite, or another crystal of unconditional love over your heart, to pour love into all the places where you have released your baggage, gently healing them, and filling them with light and love.

6. Lie quietly until you feel lighter. If you become aware of tension in any part of your body where you are holding old emotions, place the crystal over the site and allow it to dissolve the tension.

7. Let go of the past and move into whatever the present holds.

8. Thank the crystals for their work and cleanse them when it is complete.

Crystals for Your Emotions

Here is a list of crystals and the ways in which they can help you to heal emotional problems.

- **Amethyst** balances out emotional highs and lows, encouraging emotional centering. It gently dissolves emotional blocks.

- **Bloodstone** teaches you to recognize when it would be beneficial to undertake a strategic withdrawal. Encouraging you to live in the present moment, it helps move away from the past, highlighting the effect that your expectations and previous experience have on your emotional stability. It reduces irritability, impatience, and aggressiveness, and promotes selflessness.

- **Larvikite** helps you to deal flexibly with life, encouraging you not to dwell on problems. Supporting emotional healing, it goes deep into your self to release the causes of dis-ease. Larvikite assists you in seeing behind the façades people present. Keep the stone in your pocket to learn what the true desires and agendas of yourself and others are.

- **Mount Shasta Opal** infuses love into the emotional body and the mind to create a calm, quiet inner space. Useful for emotional healing at any level, it disperses stress. Placed at your throat, it helps communicate clearly and with focused intent. It is a stone of faithfulness and loyalty.

- **Porphyrite** assists you to deal with ancestral issues passed down the family line, especially involving family secrets and lies. The energetic matrix that supports the false façade is dismantled so that truth emerges. Healing, forgiveness, and reconciliation take place. Porphyrite lifts depression by deconstructing negative emotional or belief patterns and "heavy" energies that weigh on the soul. Excellent for karmic emotional healing as it works without needing to know the cause.

- **Rosophia** dissolves self-doubt and a negative self-image. De-energizing old wounds and destructive beliefs, it enables you to love yourself, showing deep compassion for all you have been through on your soul's journey.

- **Smoky Quartz** stabilizes emotions during trauma or stress, and dissolves negativity, facilitating emotional detoxification. This stone assists in tolerating difficulty times with equanimity. It relieves fear and induces emotional calm.

TODAY'S CRYSTALS

Basic: Rose Quartz

Vibration: High vibration—the "gemmier"
the crystal, the higher the vibration

- A master healer for the emotions—gentle and loving, classic heart-healer, and emotional nourisher.

- Excellent for de-stressing, soothing, and stabilizing.

- Transmutes emotional conditioning that no longer serves you.

- Strengthens empathy and sensitivity, helping you to understand how other people's feelings affect you.

- Purifies and supports forgiveness.

- Teaches how to love and value yourself.

~

Advanced: Larimar

Vibration: High

- Radiates love and peace, and promotes tranquillity.

- Effortlessly induces a deeply meditative state.

- Raises consciousness and harmonizes body and soul to new vibrations.

- Offers calm and emotional equilibrium.

- Alleviates guilt and removes fear.

- An antidote to emotional extremes and bipolar mood swings.

- Heals trauma to the heart and reconnects to joyful child energy.

- Removes self-imposed blockages and limitations.

- Dissolves self-sabotaging behavior or a tendency toward martyrdom.

- Assists taking control of life.

~

DAY 15

Crystals for Healing the Psyche and the Mind

Today's Crystals

Basic: Fluorite

Advanced: High vibration Amethysts, such as Auralite 23, Brandenberg, or Vera Cruz

Today we are going to turn our attention to crystals that heal the mind and the psyche.

Crystal energy has a powerful effect on your mind. A racing mind, mental overwhelm, or constantly going over old ground is detrimental to your well-being. There are crystals that switch off your mind—instantly. There are others that give total focus and clarity. And still others that offer fresh insights and the ability to think outside the box to find creative solutions. Simply place the appropriate crystal over a mind chakra and allow it to do its work.

Crystals interact with intention and the power of thought to potent effect. They promote clarity, concentration, focus, and creativity, and dissolve psychological dis-ease. But they also bring profound peace of mind. Over-thinking is a common cause of mental stress and the mind benefits from being switched off regularly. Some crystals contain minerals that have a naturally therapeutic effect on the mind—for example, lithium, which is prescribed for severe mood swings, is found in Kunzite and Lithium Quartz, among other stones. Factors behind psychological dis-ease, many of which involve the psyche and beliefs system, are held in the subconscious mind. Attitudes also create dis-ease and may need to be released through the appropriate chakras.

Undue mental influence, outdated concepts, and mental imperatives block a shift in consciousness or prevent you from thinking for yourself. Some of these concepts may well once have been positive, but have become fixed in your mind even though they are now past their sell-by date. Other concepts, vows, or contracts may have been set up in childhood, or in previous lives. Crystals help you to gently release these and simply allow the process to unfold in cosmic harmony (*see Day 16*).

Chakras for the Mind

Throat Chakra

Location: Center of your throat

The throat chakra is the sphere of communication. If this chakra is blocked, thoughts and feelings cannot be verbalized. Truth cannot be expressed. Other people's opinions cause difficulties. Its negative quality is mendacity, while its positive one is truthful self-expression. Typical dis-eases are active and block communication. These include sore throat/quinsy, inflammation of trachea, colds and viral infections, tinnitus and ear infections, jaw pain and gum disease, tooth problems (which relate to root beliefs), thyroid imbalances, high blood pressure, ADHD, autism, speech impediments, and psychosomatic dis-eases such as irritable bowel syndrome.

Brow (Third Eye) Chakra

Location: Above and between your eyebrows

The brow (third eye) chakra is the sphere of intuition and mental connection. Imbalances here create a sense of being bombarded by other people's thoughts, or wild and irrational intuitions that have no basis in truth. Controlling or coercing mental "hooks" from other people lock in and affect your thoughts. Its negative quality is delusion, while its positive quality is intuitive insight. Typical dis-eases are metaphysical and include migraines, mental overwhelm, schizophrenia, cataracts, iritis and other eye problems, epilepsy, autism, spinal and neurological disorders, sinus and ear infections, high blood pressure, and "irritations" of all kinds.

Crown Chakra

Location: Top of your head

This is the sphere of spiritual communication and awareness. If the crown chakra is blocked, attempting to control others is common, and if it is blown, obsession with and openness to spirit interference or possession can result. If the crown chakra is not functioning well it leads to excess environmental sensitivity and delusions or dementia. Its negative quality is arrogance, while its positive quality is spirituality. Typical dis-eases arise out of disconnection and include metabolic syndrome, vague "unwellness," nervous system disturbances, electro-magnetic and environmental sensitivity, depression, dementia, ME, insomnia or excessive sleepinesss, and disturbances of the "biological clock," such as jet lag.

Exercise: Clearing the Mind

You need: Five cleansed and activated crystals, such as Fluorite, Amethyst, or a high-vibration Amethyst such as Auralite 23 or Rhomboid Blue Selenite.

1. Lie down comfortably, ensuring that you will not be disturbed.

2. Place a mind crystal above your head (point, if it has one, facing down). Place two crystals either side of the bases of your ears.

3. Place two more crystals, one each side, equidistant between the ear crystals and the crown crystal.

4. Close your eyes and lie still for fifteen minutes. Feel the crystal energy filling your mind and quietly switching it off.

5. If you have any thoughts, let them surface but don't focus on them; let them pass by.

6. After fifteen minutes sit up and gather your crystals together.

7. Cleanse your crystals.

Useful Crystals for Your Mind

- **Auralite 23** switches off the chattering mind, instilling laser-sharp clarity and peace.

- **Bloodstone** is an excellent tonic for clearing mental overload. It reduces mental confusion and imparts mental alertness and stability. It also strengthens your ability to focus on solutions, adjusting your mindset to adapt to changing or altered circumstances.

- **Blue Lace Agate** facilitates self-expression, counteracts mental stress, and encourages your mind to expand.

- **Carnelian** enhances analytical abilities and sharpens perception. Attuning day dreamers to everyday reality, it unites logic and intuition.

- **Clear Quartz** amplifies thought power, unlocks memory, and brings about positive solutions.

- **Green Aventurine** stimulates creativity and helps you to see alternate possibilities.

- **Labradorite** balances the rational mind with intuitive wisdom.

- **Jasper** helps you get to grips with problems assertively. Combining organizational abilities with imagination, it brings hidden problems to light, helping you to find new coping strategies.

- **Rose Quartz** calms the mind and induces mental clarity.

- **Rhomboid Blue Selenite** creates a state of "no mind" by switching off mind chatter and opening the intuition to bring in higher guidance.

- **Smoky Quartz** encourages pragmatic, positive thought, applying common sense and clear insight to problems.

- **Sodalite** dispels confusion, clarifies perceptions, and releases bondage to specific ideas, encouraging the assimilation of new information. It is helpful for dyslexia and dyspraxia, as are Black Moonstone and Sugilite.

- **Yellow Labradorite (Bytownite)** switches off the conscious mind and opens the intuitive mind.

TODAY'S CRYSTALS

Basic: Fluorite

Vibration: Mid to high depending on the type of Fluorite

- Protects, especially on a psychic and psychological level.

- Enhances orderly thought, mental clarity, creativity, and clear communication.

- Clears undue mental influence.

- Aids physical and mental coordination.

- Heightens intuition.

- Wards off computer and electromagnetic stress.

Advanced: High-vibration Amethyst, such as Auralite 23, Brandenberg, or Vera Cruz
Vibration: Exceptionally high

♦ Long been used as to calm and focus the mind, improve memory, and overcome addictions.

♦ Facilitates the decision-making process, helping thinking outside the box.

♦ When gridded around the head, new high-vibration Amethysts take deep mental relaxation to a whole other level. Auralite 23 instantly switches off mind chatter, inducing laser-sharp clarity and opening the intuition. Vera Cruz Amethyst connects directly into universal consciousness (which some call the mind of God), raising consciousness to a higher level. Brandenberg Amethyst (the one crystal I wouldn't be without) dissolves old patterns and offers the highest possible guidance for inputting new ones. It contains the perfect blueprint of All That Is, opening all possibilities.

~

DAY 16

Crystals for Dissolving Old Patterns and Attachments

Today's Crystals

Basic: Flint

Advanced: Gold and Silver Healers

In addition to the chakras, the subtle electromagnetic bodies surrounding your physical body—the aura and the etheric blueprint—hold embedded patterns or have thought forms attached that may influence you. Today we're going to examine how crystals can rid you of old, outdated patterns and attachments. The aura may also have spirits connected that seek to have specific experiences through you or continue to control you. Clearing these calls for an experienced healer, but in an emergency, crystals detach spirits and send them to the light. Your etheric blueprint may hold an outdated soul intention that no longer serves you. Once these are patterns and attachments are cleared, you can literally think—and feel—for yourself.

Undue Mental Influence

Some causes of psychological dis-ease arise from outside yourself. There may be people around who feel that they know what is best for you—or what you *should* do. The intent may be well-meaning, but it is manipulative and toxic. They may have strong beliefs about you. You may pick up their thoughts and act on them, unaware of the source. Their influence can be overt or subtle, but always powerful. Strong mental conditioning may have been instilled when you were a child, and it could now unconsciously run your life. Fortunately crystals such as Fluorite, Kunzite, and Selenite help to dispel mental influence, as do Auralite 23 and other high-vibration Amethysts—wear one to protect yourself against invasion from other people's thoughts or beliefs.

Mental Constructs and Imperatives

The majority of psychological dis-ease, however, arises from within our own mind, especially those beliefs that we hold at the subconscious level, which may clash with what we think we believe. We may also be following an old soul imperative: A soul intention from another life or one that we put in place before incarnation but which is now outdated or impossible to perform.

Soul Intention

We all incarnate with a soul intention. This may be a carefully thought-out purpose for the present life, or it can be a carry-over from a past-life intention. Soul intentions are what power our spiritual evolution but if we are following an outdated intention, it can cause considerable psychological and spiritual confusion and conflict.

However, it is worth mentioning that some dis-eases, physical or psychological disturbances, have been deliberately taken on and are actually vehicles for soul growth—either for yourself or someone else. "Healing" for these dis-eases requires an understanding of the dynamics and the soul gifts that are offered by the experience. This is outside the sphere of this program (see my *Book of Why*) but it is worth bearing in mind if you are dealing with chronic dis-ease.

Past-Life Chakras

Location: Behind the ears, along the bony ridge of the skull

As we saw on Days 12 and 14, the past-life chakras are the sphere of wisdom, skills, and instinctive knowing. They contain the soul plan for your current life. They also encompass emotional baggage, unfinished business, repetitive thoughts, and outdated intentions. If the chakras are blown, you can be subconsciously overwhelmed by past-life imperatives.

Exercise: Dissolving Old Patterns

1. Stand with your feet slightly apart and "comb" all around your body—back and front—about a hand's breadth or slightly more beyond it, with a piece of Flint crystal or a Gold or Silver Healer. If a spot feels "sticky" or painful, rest the crystal there for a few moments. Spiral it out to release the energy.

2. Pay special attention to the past-life chakras behind your ears and along the bony ridge at the base of your skull.

3. Lie down comfortably and ensure you will not be disturbed.

4. Place a crystal, such as a Brandenberg Amethyst, over your brow (third eye) chakra) If you intuitively feel that past-life issues also need clearing, place other crystals either side of your ears or in the hollow at the base of your skull.

5. Ask that the crystal dissolves any thoughts, vows, beliefs, imperatives, undue mental influence, and so on that no longer serve you. Remind yourself that you don't need to know what these are. You are simply willing to release them right now.

6. Ask that the crystal dissolves any soul contracts that are no longer relevant to your spiritual growth and any outdated soul intentions for the present lifetime. Let them go with love and forgiveness. Again, you don't need to know what they are, simply be willing to relinquish them right now.

7. Then step into the karma of grace, letting go of the past and being ready to move into whatever the present holds.

8. When the process is complete, remove the crystals and thank them for their work.

9. Cleanse the crystals.

Note: Experienced crystal workers could use a Rainbow Mayanite for this process but it needs care, sensitivity, and expertise, so Gold or Silver Healers are more appropriate for when beginning this work. See also Day 17, where we explore Crystal EFT repatterning.

Useful Crystals for Cutting Ties and Detaching Spirits

- **Jasper knives** instantly cut through ties and remove entities. Dissolving old patterns, they help the etheric blueprint reconstruct to a more appropriate configuration.

- **Nirvana Quartz** reminds us that spirit attachment is one situation where informed consent is not mandatory as the soul rarely chooses to have the spirit attach. This crystal is particularly useful for spirit-release work in which a friend or a relative acts as the intermediary.

Additional stones may be needed to seal the aura against re-invasion.

- **Rainbow Mayanite** is the finest tool there is for working in the subtle etheric layers to remove ties and attachments, but it should only be used by an experienced crystal healer. It blends particularly well with Petaltone Plant Ally and Special 8 essences.

- **Stibnite** creates an energetic shield around the physical body. It separates out the pure from the dross and is an efficient tool for releasing entity possession or negative energy. Eliminating tentacles from clingy relationships, it assists in tie-cutting rituals and past-life release.

TODAY'S CRYSTALS

Basic: Flint
Vibration: Earthy

- A powerful stabilizer and cleanser.
- Calls guides and power allies to you.

- Protective and turns back curses and ill-wishing.

- Hones the spirit and cuts away all that is outworn and outgrown, slicing through psychological blockages, problems, and ties etherically linking people.

- Dissolves chakra cords and heals the site.

~

Advanced: Gold and Silver Healers
Vibration: Very high

- Come from the same mine as Rainbow Mayanite, and are beautifully iridescent and soothing.

- Gently dissolve ties and undue influences, removing entities and sending them to the light—even at a distance.

- Do excellent deep repair work on the light body, chakras, aura, and intercellular structures. Packed with bioscalar waves.

- Particularly useful for those with sensitive auras, or beginners.

- See also Rainbow Mayanite (*see Day 17*).

~

DAY 17

Crystals for Inputting New Patterns

Today's Crystals

Basic: Brandenberg or other high-vibration Amethyst
Advanced: Rainbow Mayanite

The easiest way I have found to input new patterns is through Crystal EFT (Emotional Freedom Technique), which is a process involving tapping on specific points of the body to take out an old pattern and replace it with a constructive, soul-appropriate pattern. This is our focus for today.

Crystal EFT is a variation of the Emotional Freedom Technique in which you tap on specific points on the energetic meridians of your body to clear negative emotions, toxic thoughts, and destructive behavior patterns—and to instil a new pattern. Tapping with a crystal such as a Brandenberg Amethyst, a Gold or a Silver Healer, or a Rainbow Mayanite dramatically heightens the transformation as the crystal transmutes the negativity that is released during the tapping.

When working with Crystal EFT, follow your instincts and allow yourself to say anything that comes to mind, no matter how ludicrous or unlikely it may sound. This "free-flow stream of consciousness" combined with loving and forgiving acceptance of yourself is the way to uncover, release, and transform your deepest fears, ingrained thoughts, anger, toxic emotions, and beliefs that lurk in the depths of your subconscious mind. It is the one time when it pays—initially—to be as negative as you possibly can be.

Although the instructions are to tap on each point seven times, it really doesn't matter if you do six or eight as you'll get into your own rhythm as you tap. It can be quite confusing when you first start trying to count, tap, and say your statement all at the same time, but don't worry. That's part of why it works! It takes you out of your rational, everyday mind and allows the emotions and feelings to surface so, in a way, the more confused you are the better. Just keep following the process.

In addition to transmuting negative energy, a crystal such as a Brandenberg Amethyst or a Rainbow Mayanite restores your subtle energy grid to the perfect energetic state it had before a pattern, thought, or emotion became ingrained. This is why Crystal EFT adds in an extra tapping point, the soma chakra, that links to that perfect energy grid. Whichever crystal you use, ensure you cleanse and dedicate it before use and cleanse it afterward.

Points are tapped with the flat or rounded end rather than point of the crystal to avoid possibility of injury.

The Tapping Points

1. "Karate chop": Outer edge of the hand.

2. Crown chakra: Top of the head.

3. Soma chakra: Center of the forehead at the hairline.

4. Brow (third eye): Center of the forehead slightly above the eyebrows.

5. Inner corner of the eyebrow.

6. Outer corner of the eyebrow.

7. Below the center of the eye.

8. Below the nose.

9. Center of the chin.

10. "Sore spot" on collar bone either side of the breastbone.

11. Spleen chakra, a hand's breadth below the left armpit.

Useful additional points for emotional or spiritual pain and mental or emotional baggage:

1. "Spirit ground:" Either side of your breastbone about a hand's breadth beneath your collar bone—just above the breasts in women and slightly higher than the nipples in men.

2. "Baggage" point: Half-way along the top of your shoulder (tap with all your fingers and you'll soon find it). Tap both shoulders.

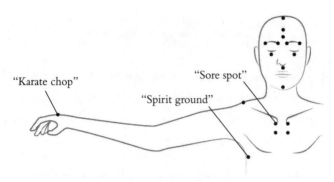

"Karate chop"

"Sore spot"

"Spirit ground"

The Tapping Points

The Set-up Statement

The set-up statement identifies the core issue or feelings you're working on. From a stream-of-consciousness rant, something key emerges. You may be surprised at what you're really angry or sad about—small triggers release huge wells of ancient anger and pain. If this happens, go with it, keep talking, and continue tapping.

Your set-up statement will probably be along the lines of "I've always felt angry... neglected... fouled things up... never chosen the right partner..."

Your personal set-up statement is always followed by: "Nevertheless I deeply and profoundly love, accept, and forgive myself unconditionally and completely."

Exercise: Crystal Tapping

Follow the stages below using the tapping points on whichever side of the body feels comfortable. Allow your intuition and the crystal to guide the order in which you tap —or indeed the places that you tap

1. Find your set-up statement by tapping seven times on each point and allowing your mind to tell you what you are holding on to; what negative patterns are buried deep in your subconscious mind. Don't censor, just rant.

2. Then formulate your set-up statement. For example: "Even though I always seem to have let people abuse and misuse me and let me down and betray me, I nevertheless deeply and completely love, accept, and forgive myself."

3. Saying your initial set-up statement out loud and holding the crystal against the palm of your hand with your thumb, tap against the "karate chop" point on the side of the other hand seven times or whatever feels right to you. Repeat your set-up statement several times while tapping, allowing whatever words come into your mind to be spoken.

4. Chose a word or a short phrase that is shorthand for your issue. It may change as you move through the

points, so allow whatever needs to be said to come out of your mouth. Reassure yourself that there is no right way to do this–you can do and say whatever works for you. For example, you could say: "Let down, betrayed, and misused."

5. Hold your crystal between your forefinger and thumb. Saying your shorthand phrase out loud and starting with the top of your head, tap each point (one side only or both as you feel is appropriate) seven times or so with the flat side of the crystal if it has a point or the rounded end if it is tumbled. Allow your hand to move freely between the points if this feels appropriate–you may want to tap in a reverse direction once you've reach the spleen point, for example.

6. Check out how you are feeling. If necessary, tap all the points for two more rounds allowing changes in the wording to emerge as you tap. Cleanse your crystal if this feels appropriate.

7. Rephrase your initial set-up statement to allow for change and to become more positive. For example: "I am in control of my life and open to being loved deeply and fully. I deeply and completely love, accept, and forgive myself."

8. "Karate chop" the side of your hand seven times or so while repeating this new statement out loud, again allowing any changes or unconscious phrases to be spoken but adding the final phrase.

9. Using a more positive shorthand phrase or anything that comes to mind as you move between points, do another round of tapping on each point following the instinct of your hand guided by the crystal.

10. Repeat two more rounds of tapping if necessary, allowing changes in wording to emerge spontaneously as you tap.

11. Make the third and final statement as positive as possible, finding the opposite to your original feeling.

12. Do another round of tapping saying your final shorthand phrase, and again finish with: "And I deeply and profoundly love, accept, and forgive myself unconditionally and completely."

13. Sit quietly for a few moments reviewing how you feel and enjoying the change you've brought about. If you're using a Brandenberg Amethyst or a Rainbow Mayanite, place it over your heart as you do this.

14. Cleanse your crystal.

TODAY'S CRYSTALS

Basic: Brandenberg Amethyst
Vibration: Extremely high

- Holds the perfect blueprint of All That Is.

- Repatterns all the subtle layers and levels of being, imprinting the most perfect pattern possible.

~

Advanced: Rainbow Mayanite
Vibration: Exceptionally high

- Offers rainbow chakra healing and the activation of new joy, ascension, focus, purpose, and stepping on to your true path.

- Contains immense quantities of natural bioscalar healing waves.

- De-energizes old patterns from any source, taking out the debris and karmic encrustations from the past.

- Pulls out any toxic dross absorbed from other people or the environment.

- Builds new and more supportive structures.

- Takes you into the depths of yourself to how your soul is manoeuvring you onto your pathway and how an apparently detrimental situation offers you soul gifts.

- Offers enormous support during change through its iron content.

~

DAY 18

Crystals for Opening Higher Consciousness

Today's Crystals

Basic: Selenite

Advanced: Aurora Quartz (Anandalite™)

Crystals are a wonderful source of strength during times of change, but where they really come into their own is in bringing about a vibrational shift of consciousness, literally taking us into a new dimension—or rather opening all possible dimensions. Today we explore how crystals can help us open our higher consciousness.

There are many crystals available now whose stated aim is to usher in a "new age" of elevated awareness and integrated perception of being both human and divine at the same time: Unity consciousness. But the crystals also point out that we cannot achieve this unity until we have completed our personal healing and growth work.

High-vibration chakras are coming on line as energy shifts occur. These chakras assist in assimilating the changing frequencies, and exploring other dimensions. If you are a beginner, this higher chakra activation is best done slowly: Work on one chakra at a time until you are sure that it is functioning well, before you move on to the next one. But if you have been raising your vibrations already, your chakras may have opened spontaneously.

The Higher Chakras

Heart Seed Chakra

Location: Base of breastbone

This chakra governs soul remembrance. It recalls the reason for this incarnation, your connection to the Divine plan, and accesses tools available to manifest potential. If it is blown or blocked, you will feel rootless, purposeless, or lost.

Higher Heart Chakra

Location: Above the heart

This is the chakra of unconditional love. It is forgiving, accepting, and spiritually connected. If it is blown or blocked, you will be spiritually disconnected, grieving, or needy.

Soma Chakra

Location: Above the brow (third eye); at the hairline

This chakra is the seat of spiritual connection and is where your subtle bodies, including the light body, attach themselves. When it is functioning well, you will be spiritually aware and fully conscious, but if it is blown or blocked you will feel cut off from spiritual nourishment and connection and make an easy target for discarnate spirits to attach themselves to.

Soul Star Chakra

Location: Above your head

This chakra governs spiritual enlightenment and illumination. It is the ultimate soul connection, offering an objective perspective on the past. If it is blown or blocked, it can lead to spiritual arrogance, soul fragmentation, spirit attachment, and extra vulnerability to psychic attack.

Stellar Gateway Chakra

Location: Above the Soul Star

This chakra is the cosmic doorway to other worlds and communication with enlightened beings. If it is blown or blocked, you are open to illusions—a source of cosmic disinformation that leads to delusion, deception, and disintegration, leaving you unable to function in the everyday world.

The Alta Major Chakra

Location: Inside the skull

This chakra is a major factor in accelerating and expanding consciousness. The anchor for the multi-dimensional light body, it unites metaphysical sight and intuitive insight. It holds valuable information about our ancestral past and the ingrained patterns that have governed human life and awareness. This chakra contains your past-life karma and the contractual agreements you made with your higher self and others before incarnating in this lifetime. Activating it enables you to read your soul's plan.

It creates a complex, *merkaba*-like geometric shape within and around the skull that stretches from the base of the skull to the crown, connecting the past life and soma chakras, hippocampus, hypothalamus, and pineal and pituitary glands with the brow (third eye) and the higher crown chakras. Its link to the throat chakra facilitates expression of information from higher dimensions. Its positive function is to create a direct pathway to your subconscious and your intuitive mind. It also allows you to instinctively know your spiritual purpose. Reputedly the alta major chakra has been imprinted with "divine codes" that, when activated, allow cosmic evolution to fully manifest on Earth. High-vibration crystals activate these codes. Imbalances in this chakra show as eye problems (floaters, cataracts), migraine headaches, feelings of confusion, "dizziness" or "floatiness," loss of sense of purpose, and spiritual depression.

Exercise:
Higher Chakra Activation

The activation should be carried out with the basic chakras cleansed and open.

Note: Open these chakras slowly and in order. Do not rush the process.

1. Place a higher heart chakra crystal, such as Danburite, Rose Quartz, or Tugtupite, over the higher heart chakra and leave it in place for two to five minutes. This chakra can be left open.

2. Place a higher heart chakra crystal over the heart seed chakra at the base of the breastbone and feel the influx of universal love that floods into the chakra and through your whole being. This chakra can be left open.

3. Place a Preseli Bluestone or other cosmic anchor crystal, such as Flint, over the soma chakra. Open the chakra when you want to go journeying (see Day 19) and close it when you want to stay in your physical body.

4. Place a high-vibration crystal, such as Aurora Quartz (Anandalite™), Azeztulite, Rainbow Mayanite, or Selenite, on the soul star chakra to connect you to your soul and highest self. Invoke your higher self to guard it well. Close

the chakra when not using the portal for journeying (*see Day 19*) or guidance.

5. Before opening the stellar gateway chakra, invoke your guardian angel or other protective being to guard it well while you journey or seek guidance in other realms. Place Aurora Quartz (Anandalite™), Rainbow Mayanite, or Selenite here to open the portal. Close the portal and the chakra when you have completed your journey.

6. Use Aurora Quartz (Anandalite™) to activate the alta major chakra. Place in the hollow at the base of the skull.

7. Remember to close the chakras when the exercise is complete. To close your chakras, remove the crystal and place your hand over the site to close a high-vibration chakra down. You can also picture chakra shutters closing over it or place a piece of Flint over the chakra.

TODAY'S CRYSTALS

Basic: Selenite
Vibration: High

- ◆ Crystallized Divine light.

- ◆ Connects to All That Is.

- ◆ Brings clarity of mind and accesses angelic consciousness.

- ◆ Anchors light body in the Earth vibration.

- ◆ Instils deep peace.

- ◆ Inhabits the place between light and matter.

- ◆ Pinpoints lessons and issues from other lives still being worked upon.

- ◆ Powerful stabilizer for erratic emotions.

~

Advanced: Aurora Quartz (Anandalite™)
Vibration: Exceedingly high

- ◆ Harmonizes the light body into the Earth vibration through its natural iridescent rainbows.

- Prepares the central nervous system for a vibrational shift.

- Contains a massive amount of bioscalar waves.

- Activates psychic and physical immune systems.

- Purifies and aligns whole chakra system to higher frequencies.

- Strips you to the bare bones of your soul and rebuilds your energy patterns to accommodate a massive energy shift into enlightenment on Earth.

- Deconstructs detrimental energy structures and restructures appropriately for consciousness shift.

- Takes you into the interconnectedness of all life for a quantum uplift.

- Introduces the limitless possibilities of multi-dimensional being.

~

DAY 19

Meditation and Journeying with Crystals

Today's Crystals

Basic: Preseli Bluestone
Advanced: Brandenberg Amethyst

Today we explore the crystals that are useful for meditation and journeying (making a spiritual journey through visualization).

High-vibration crystals raise your vibrations, enabling effortless multi- and inter-dimensional journeying, especially when combined in grids. But common sense must prevail and you need to be anchored at the same time. This grid takes you into extremely high dimensions and permanently changes your energetic frequency so that you resonate in sync with the highest potential of the changing times. Alternative crystals are given so find the ones best attuned to your own unique vibrations (*see Day 1*). If you are fairly new to crystal working, the opaque forms of high-vibration crystals take you into raised vibrations more gently. Build this grid slowly, allowing yourself to attune to and assimilate the energy of each of the crystals as the chakras open. Before journeying, ensure that you are in a safe space (*see Day 9*).

Exercise: Grow Your Shamanic Anchor

A shamanic anchor holds you gently in incarnation, so it's a good idea to put one in place before meditation or journeying.

1. Picture two roots coming out of the base of your spine and down your legs. They pass through the soles of your feet and unite at the earth star chakra, a foot (30cm) or so below which they twine together into a strong cord. This flexible cord grows down through the crust of the Earth into the molten magma until it reaches the iron ball at the core.

2. Hook your shamanic anchor onto that ball. It always brings you back safely to your body.

Shamanic anchor crystals: Boji Stones; Elestial Smoky Quartz; Graphic Smoky Quartz; Hematite; Smoky Quartz; Stibnite.

Exercise: Grow Your Cosmic Anchor

A cosmic anchor helps your light body and soul find their way back to the physical body, assisting you to journey safely through multi-dimensions and know your way back.

1. Place your crystal on the soma chakra (on your hairline above the third eye, above and between your eyebrows). The cosmic anchor also helps connect to your higher self, the part that is not fully in incarnation and which, therefore, sees much further.

2. From your soma chakra feel a silver cord growing outward and upward. This cord passes up through the higher chakras, meeting your higher self. From your higher self the cosmic anchor passes through the outer layer of the Earth's mantle and into space. In the constellation of Sagittarius, it hooks itself onto the tip of the archer's arrow where the galactic center is located. It keeps you balanced between Earth and cosmos, spirit and matter, and always shows you the way home to your body.

Cosmic anchor crystals: Brandenberg Amethyst; Flint; Preseli Bluestone; Selenite; Stibnite; Tantalite; or high-vibration Quartzes (Aurora (Anandalite™); Brandenberg; Rainbow Mayanite; Satyaloka; Satyamani; or Trigonic).

Exercise: The Cosmic Runway

The layout starts with your feet so that you are well grounded (you will be lying down by the time you place the crystals over your head). It can be useful to set a quiet signal or alarm for 20 minutes' time to call you back. This particular layout takes you journeying through other dimensions but can be adapted for meditation or for journeying through the shamanic worlds—use Flint, Preseli Bluestone, and Stibnite rather than high-vibration Quartzes for a shamanic journey. Use high-vibration crystals for a meditation layout, but tell yourself that you will stay with your body and attract celestial energies to yourself.

You will need:

- A grounding crystal such as Elestial Smoky Quartz or Hematite.

- Anchor crystals such as Boji Stones; Elestial Quartz; Flint; Graphic Smoky Quartz; Hematite, Preseli Bluestone; Selenite; Smoky Brandenberg Amethyst; or Smoky Elestial Quartz.

- Alta major chakra crystals such as Aurora Quartz (Anandalite™) or Blue Moonstone.

- High-vibration crystals such as Aurora Quartz (Anandalite™); Azeztulite; Brandenberg Amethyst; Petalite; Phenacite; Nirvana Quartz; Rainbow Mayanite; Satyaloka Quartz; Satyamani Quartz; or Selenite.

Once you're ready, you can begin the layout:

1. Lie in a warm comfortable place so that you can place the crystals on the ground around yourself, or ask a friend to do this for you.

2. Place a Smoky Elestial Quartz or other shamanic anchor crystal slightly below and between your feet and consciously invoke your shamanic anchor (*see page 162*). Tell yourself that your body will remain grounded and centered while you explore other dimensions and that you will return after 20 minutes.

3. Place two high-vibration crystals at your hips where you can put your hands on them (Flint or Stibnite for a shamanic journey).

4. Place a high-vibration crystal level with or slightly below your shoulders (Flint or Stibnite for a shamanic journey).

5. Place a high-vibration crystal at the top of your head (not necessary for a shamanic journey). Consciously invoke your cosmic anchor.

6. Place a high-vibration crystal about a foot above your head (not necessary for a shamanic journey). Feel the soul star chakra open.

7. Place Aurora Quartz (Anandalite™) or Rainbow Mayanite as high as you can reach above your head (not necessary for a shamanic journey). Feel the stellar gateway chakra open.

8. Place an alta major chakra opener in the hollow at the base of your skull (not necessary for a shamanic journey).

9. Close your eyes, relax, and place your Brandenberg Amethyst, Preseli Bluestone, or other cosmic anchor crystal on the soma chakra at your hairline. Put your hands on the crystals at your hips. Feel yourself lifting out of your physical body into your light body.

10. Allow the crystals to take you journeying to your destination.

11. When it is time to return, slide down your cosmic anchor and settle into your body once more. Take the crystal off your soma chakra. Feel your light body settling back into your body, which realigns its energies to accommodate the new frequencies.

12. Lift your hand up and remove the Aurora Quartz (Anandalite™), put it to one side, and picture the stellar gateway chakra closing.

13. Put the soul star crystal to one side, feeling the soul star chakra closing.

14. Remove the alta major chakra crystal from the base of your skull.

15. Sit up slowly. Put the other crystals to one side in the reverse order to which you laid them out. Check that your body has realigned to the new energy and the light body is incorporated into your physical being. (Aurora Quartz on your soma chakra helps to assimilate and integrate the new energies).

16. When you reach the Elestial Quartz, put your hands on the crystal and check that your shamanic anchor is in place. If you need to integrate the changes, keep your hands on the crystal and ask it to assist assimilation. Sit quietly allowing the process to complete itself.

17. Thank the crystals for their work.

18. Stand up slowly, stamp your feet, and have a warm drink.

Today's Crystals

Basic: Preseli Bluestone
Vibration: Earthy and high

- A healing stone of the ancestors and a visionary crystal.

- Grounds and focuses.

- Ideal for journeying as there is an inbuilt sense of direction.

- Creates unshakeable inner core energetic solidity to stabilize you through Earth changes.

- Acts as a battery: Generating, earthing, and grounding spiritual energy and power, and enhancing psychic ability and metaphysical gifts.

~

Advanced: Brandenberg Amethyst or Auralite 23 *(see Day 17)*

- Takes you through the multi-dimensions of being.

~

DAY 20

Crystals for Earth Healing

Today's Crystals

Basic: Aragonite

Advanced: Smoky Elestial Quartz

We humans take so much from our planet, so today we're going to learn how to give something back by using crystals for Earth healing.

Crystals transmute and heal areas of disturbance and repair the Earth's energetic grid. They can be placed directly onto the ground or on maps to restore equilibrium to an area. They also protect and create sacred space. Remember to cleanse them regularly. Earth imbalances are caused by factors such as geopollutants, mining, nuclear testing, and the shifting of the tectonic plates of the planet during earthquakes, or by the energetic imprint of events that took place at a site. Your connection to the earth beneath your feet is through the earth star chakra.

The Earth Star Chakra

Location: A foot (30cm) or so below the feet

The earth star is the chakra of material connection. When your earth star chakra is in balance, you are well grounded, able to operate effectively in everyday reality, and can intuit Earth imbalances. However, when it is out of balance, you feel ungrounded, you are impractical, and you pick up negative impressions of what has previously occurred at a site, spirits of place, or stuck spirits. If your chakra is permanently open, you easily assimilate negative energies from the ground or from events that have taken place.

The Earth's Chakra System

The Earth's chakra system links sites around the planet. Chakras can cover vast distances radiating out from a central sacred site. Not everyone agrees on exactly where these chakras are located. Additional Earth chakras are coming on line to assimilate higher vibrational energies and over

156 were identified by Earth-chakra specialist and author Robert Coon. Earth healing at the chakras and other vortex points opens, purifies, aligns, and heals the Earth's energy field, revitalizes the Earth's energetic matrix, and maintains overall planetary well-being.

The Seven Major Earth Chakras

- **Base:** Mount Shasta, California, USA (alternatives: Grand Canyon, Arizona, USA; Black Mesa, Sedona, Arizona, USA).

- **Sacral:** Lake Titicaca, Peru and Bolivia, (alternatives: Machu Picchu, Peru; Amazon River, Peru, Colombia, and Brazil).

- **Solar plexus:** Uluru, Australia

- **Heart:** Glastonbury, UK (alternative: River Ganges, India)

- **Throat:** Great Pyramid of Giza, Egypt

- **Brow (Third Eye):** Mount Fuji, Japan (alternative: Kuh-e Malek Siah, Iran)

- **Crown:** Mount Kailash, Tibet

Gridding

As we have seen (*Day 13*), gridding is the art of placing crystals to restore equilibrium, whether to a site or to the Earth itself. You do not have to visit a site as the layout can be done on a map. Remember to allow energy to flow through you to harness the power of the crystal. Do not use your own energy.

Useful Earth Healing Grid Shapes

Zig-zag

The zig-zag layout is particularly useful for sick-building syndrome and for transmuting environmental pollution. Place appropriate crystals as shown on the diagram below, remembering to return from the last stone laid to the first immediately after laying them out. Cleanse regularly.

Zig-zag Grid

Triangulation

Triangulation neutralizes negative energy and brings in positive energy. This grid is particularly useful for healing a site, restoring its energies to equilibrium, or for protection. If placing crystals at a site or on a map, dowse for the right position for the crystals (*see Day 1*). When gridding a room, place one crystal centrally along a wall and two others on the wall opposite with equal angles if possible. If doing a whole house, the lines of force pass through walls. Connect the points with a wand to strengthen the grid. You can also use the six-pointed star grid (*see Day 13*).

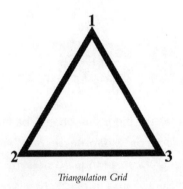

Triangulation Grid

Five-pointed star

This is a powerful Earth-healer formation, particularly suitable for map work. Follow the direction of the arrows on the diagram when placing your crystals and remember to walk back to the start crystal to complete the circuit.

Five-pointed Star Grid

Exercise:
Healing Ancient Earth Trauma

Choose a site where there has been a battle, a massacre, or another event, or where there has been significant Earth-trauma, such as an earthquake or tsunami. Find a map of the site sufficiently large to place crystals on it or visit the site itself.

You need: Five Aragonite or other Earth-healing stones, one Smoky Elestial Quartz, and a crystal wand

1. Dowse to find your starting point above the site (or use north) and place an Aragonite crystal on that spot.

2. Move down to the right (as you look at the map or walk the site) and place an Aragonite below and to the side of the site.

3. Move up and to the left and place an Aragonite above and to the side of the site.

4. Move across and to the right and place an Aragonite to encompass the site.

5. Move down and to the left to place the final Aragonite.

6. Join up the five-pointed star with a wand, ensuring that you return to the first crystal laid.

7. Place a Smoky Elestial Quartz in the center.

8. Ask that the trauma, energetic pollution, or disturbance be transmuted and brought back into equilibrium.

9. Leave the map with the crystals in place to do their healing work or leave the crystals where you placed them at the site.

10. When completed, if using a map, dismantle the star and send any residual healing to the Earth. Otherwise leave the crystals in place at the site to maintain the energy.

Note: You can lay the same configuration over one of the Earth's chakras to help restore the Earth's energetic grid. Other Elestial Quartzes, such as Amethyst, Clear, or Rose, bring in unconditional love to an area.

TODAY'S CRYSTALS

Basic: Aragonite

Vibration: Earthy to high depending on color and type (brown Aragonite is earthy; lilac and blue very high).

- Grounding and healing.

- Transforms geopathic stress and blocked ley lines.

- Deepens connection with the Earth.

- Combines well with Halite (powerfully cleansing), Black Tourmaline (absorbs negativity, calms disturbance), and Flint (stabilizes the ground).

Advanced: Smoky Elestial Quartz

Vibration: Exceedingly high, as with all elestials

- One of the finest transmutors of negative energy.

- A powerful catalyst for change—its shifts are immensely fast but it holds equilibrium within the changes.

- Restructures energy fields and facilitates cellular healing while working at multi-dimensional levels.

- Grounds grids into everyday reality or anchors healings for the body or Earth.

- Pulls negative energy out of the environment, transmutes it, and protects the whole area.

- Reframes the etheric blueprint and ancestral line, so that cellular memory is reprogrammed and power restored to future generations.

- Releases karmic group enmeshment where the same patterns repeat life after life.

- Assists spirit release work.

- Blocks the effects of geopathic stress when gridded around a bed.

~

DAY 21

Living the Crystal Way

Today's Crystals

Your crystal collection

We've reached the last day so it's time today to bring all your crystal knowledge together and integrate it into your life.

Once you attune to crystal energy the changes in your consciousness are rapid and your life opens out in unexpected ways. Many years ago I wrote:

> *And finally, if you want to change your life, find yourself one of the new Shift Crystals. These amazing, high-energy crystals were formed from Quartz that was laid down on Calcite. The Calcite*

then dissolved away leaving fissures and caverns
studded with beautiful crystals. When one was first
put into my hand, I simply could not let go. For years
I used a visualization of traveling into a crystal cave
when leading meditations to find our soul purpose.
Now that crystal cave was in my hand and I could
feel all my old programming dropping away and
the energies quite literally shifting as I attuned to
my purpose. It was a moment for which I had been
preparing all my life.

It brought about profound—and rapid—changes, some welcome, others not so at the time. But all were purposeful and part of my spiritual evolution. Sadly, as with so many crystals that come into play for a short time, they do their work, and then retire. There are very few Shift Crystals around these days (but I still have my crystal cave and you can tune into its vibrations from afar). However, fortunately many of the new high-vibration finds have taken over that role and have lifted my energies—and my understanding—way beyond what I'd have thought was possible back then. I look on it as an ever-expanding ladder of crystal energies that reaches into multi-dimensions and opens infinite possibilities.

So, how do you integrate crystal energy? Here are some ideas.

1. Play with your crystals! Spend joyful time with them; meditate and listen to what they have to say. Attune to the crystal mentors (*see page 182*) and they will guide your life and your spiritual evolution—if you allow them to.

2. Wear your crystals. Let them impart their energies and raise your vibrations on a daily basis.

3. Surround yourself with just enough crystals. Don't overdo it!!! (Anyone who has been in my home will laugh at this, but you need to find the right number of harmonious crystals for you.) Use crystal grids for safe and sacred space, protection, and energy enhancement.

4. Whenever you feel slightly off balance, ask your crystals which one wants to work with you to bring back equilibrium and offer you healing.

5. Be open to new crystals finding you. The majority of my most exciting crystals have arrived serendipitously. Turn on your heart light and draw them to you.

Exercise: Meeting the Crystal Mentors

All crystals have "higher beings," or crystal oversouls, which hold the energy of the specific crystal-type and which communicate with and guide you in your crystal work. These crystal mentors are anxious to make contact.

1. Sit comfortably and hold your crystal in your hands or put it where you can comfortably gaze into it.

2. Invite the crystal oversoul to make itself known to you.

3. Half-close your eyes and gaze at the crystal.

4. Open your brow (third eye) chakra and feel the crystal energy taking it to a higher frequency. Feel yourself wrapped in crystal love.

5. Be open to the crystal oversoul communicating with you through images, intuitions, thoughts, impressions, feelings, or bodily sensations.

6. When you have finished, thank the crystal oversoul for its guidance and break off contact, but be aware that you can reconnect at any time.

Afterword

Now you've had a taste of what crystal energies can do, where do you go from here with your crystals? Well, you may like to go back to uses with which you have particularly resonated, say Earth healing or consciousness raising, and repeat the activities with several different crystals. However, if you're new to crystal work, you could fruitfully spend several days on each exercise trying out various crystals until you feel you have really grasped it. Or, if you want to explore a particular crystal application in depth, you could happily spend 21 days developing just one day's activities further by exploring how you and 21 different crystals respond to that particular exercise. Or indeed how only one crystal responds to all the days' activities. Just remember that, whatever you do, crystals work best when helping and healing everyone for the highest good of all.

So, for instance, let's say you want to use your crystals for healing yourself and your family or your environment. The key here is to find a crystal—or crystals—that resonates with you, which immediately makes you feel good and induces a sense of well-being, and then to remember to use it at the first sign of dis-ease. You could put together a "crystal first-aid kit" that you keep with you. Mine has Quantum Quattro, Que Sera, Red Jasper, Cathedral Quartz (for pain), Shungite and Bloodstone (anti-bacterial and anti-viral), Smoky Quartz (to draw off negativity), and any other crystal that asks to join me on my travels. I pop in a bottle of crystal cleanser and I'm covered for most eventualities. But I only work on other people when they ask me to or when I have the permission of their higher self.

Similarly I have a traveling "Earth healing kit" as I find so many places need their energies cleansing and restoring. It's got Aragonite, Black Tourmaline, Rhodozite, Selenite, and Smoky Quartz on call, along with an appropriate wand. I always call in the crystal oversouls to help in this work and you will find that helpful too. Now that you've learned to sense energies and to put them back into equilibrium, you'll find that you can quietly do a great deal of good work in this way. A peaceful, safe, and harmonious environment is one of the greatest gifts you can offer those around you and the planet.

If you want to use your crystals to raise your consciousness, have them with you whenever you meditate or journey. They will effortlessly lift your vibrations and will assist in assimilating the information and "upgrades" you are given. Remember that this work needs to be grounded in order to function here on the earth-plane, rather remaining in Woo-Woo Land where it all sounds very lovely but doesn't actually make any difference to everyday reality. The crystals will be only too eager to expand their properties and possibilities the more you work with them, and opportunities will open up the more aware you yourself become. Personally, I believe that the consciousness of the whole can only shift when each person individually does their own inner work—rather than trying to heal someone "out there." So, concentrate your efforts on expanding your awareness, clearing out your blocks, sorting out your karma, and integrating the new energies that the crystals offer you. They will open your eyes to a whole new world.

Don't forget that the most important key to good crystal work is to use crystals that have been cleansed, blessed, and asked to work with you for the highest good of all, and which resonate with you at every level of your being. Start with clean crystals and the rest will follow.

Be flexible and find the right way for you!

Enjoy your crystals,

Judy Hall

Resources

Books by Judy Hall

Crystals for Energy Protection, Hay House, 2020 (previously published as *Crystals for Psychic Self-protection*, Hay House, 2014 and *Psychic Self-protection*, Hay House, 2009)

Crystals Made Easy, Hay House, 2018 (previously published as *Crystals (Hay House Basics),* Hay House, 2015

The Crystal Companion, Godsfield Press, 2018

Crystal Grids, Fair Winds Press, 2018

Psychic Development, Flying Horse Press, 2014

Earth Blessings, Watkins Books, 2014

The Crystal Wisdom Oracle, Watkins Books, 2013

Crystals and Sacred Sites, Fair Winds Press, 2012

The Encyclopedia of Crystals (Revised), Godsfield Press and Fair Winds Press, 2012

The Crystal Bible, Volumes I, ll and III, Godsfield Press, 2003, 2009 and 2012

101 Power Crystals, Fair Winds Press, 2011

Life-changing Crystals, Godsfield Press, 2011

The Book of Why, Flying Horse Press, 2010

The Soulmate Myth, Flying Horse Press, 2010

Crystal Experience, Godsfield Press, 2010

Good Vibrations, Flying Horse Press, 2008

Crystal Love, Godsfield Press, 2007

Crystal Prescriptions Volumes 1–8, O-Books, 2005–2019

Crystal Healing, Godsfield Press, 2005

The Astrology Bible, Godsfield Press, 2005

Torn Clouds, O-Books, 2005 (fiction)

The Crystal Zodiac, Godsfield Press, 2004

Crystal Suppliers

www.exquisitecrystals.com (USA)

www.ksccrystals.com (UK)

www.hehishelo.co.uk (UK)

Cleansers

Clear2Light from Petaltone is an excellent crystal cleanser and is available worldwide at www.petaltone.co.uk (UK) or www.petaltoneusa.com (USA).

Online Courses

Crystals Made Easy, Hay House, 2015

About the Author

Judy Hall was an internationally recognized author, crystal expert, astrologer, psychic, healer, broadcaster, and workshop leader. She held a BEd in Religious Studies and a Masters Degree in Cultural Astronomy and Astrology, and had an extensive knowledge of world religions and mythology. Her numerous books, including the million-selling *The Crystal Bible*, have been translated into 18 languages.

Bonus Content

Thank you for purchasing *21 Days to Work with Crystals* by Judy Hall. This product includes a free download! To access this bonus content, please visit www.hayhouse.com/download and enter the Product ID and Download Code as they appear below:

Product ID: 3965
Download Code: ebook

For further assistance, please contact Hay House Customer Care by phone: US (800) 654-5126 or INTL CC+(760) 431-7695 or visit www.hayhouse.com/contact.

Thank you again for your Hay House purchase. Enjoy!

Hay House, Inc. • P.O. Box 5100 • Carlsbad, CA 92018 • (800) 654-5126

Caution: This audio program features meditation/visualization exercises that render it inappropriate for use while driving or operating heavy machinery.

Publisher's note: Hay House products are intended to be powerful, inspirational, and life-changing tools for personal growth and healing. They are not intended as a substitute for medical care. Please use this audio program under the supervision of your care provider. Neither the authors nor Hay House, Inc., assume any responsibility for your improper use of this product.

We hope you enjoyed this Hay House book. If you'd like to receive our online catalog featuring additional information on Hay House books and products, or if you'd like to find out more about the Hay Foundation, please contact:

Hay House, Inc., P.O. Box 5100, Carlsbad, CA 92018-5100
(760) 431-7695 or (800) 654-5126
(760) 431-6948 (fax) or (800) 650-5115 (fax)
www.hayhouse.com® • www.hayfoundation.org

———

Published in Australia by: Hay House Australia Pty. Ltd.,
18/36 Ralph St., Alexandria NSW 2015
Phone: 612-9669-4299 • *Fax:* 612-9669-4144
www.hayhouse.com.au

Published in the United Kingdom by: Hay House UK, Ltd.,
The Sixth Floor, Watson House, 54 Baker Street, London W1U 7BU
Phone: +44 (0)20 3927 7290 • *Fax:* +44 (0)20 3927 7291
www.hayhouse.co.uk

Published in India by: Hay House Publishers India,
Muskaan Complex, Plot No. 3, B-2, Vasant Kunj, New Delhi 110 070
Phone: 91-11-4176-1620 • *Fax:* 91-11-4176-1630
www.hayhouse.co.in

———

Access New Knowledge.
Anytime. Anywhere.

Learn and evolve at your own pace
with the world's leading experts.

www.hayhouseU.com

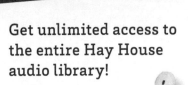

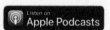

CONNECT WITH

HAY HOUSE

ONLINE

🌐 hayhouse.co.uk   **f** @hayhouse

📷 @hayhouseuk   🐦 @hayhouseuk

▶ @hayhouseuk   ♪ @hayhouseuk

Find out all about our latest books & card decks • Be the first to know about exclusive discounts • Interact with our authors in live broadcasts • Celebrate the cycle of the seasons with us • Watch free videos from your favourite authors • Connect with like-minded souls

'*The gateways to wisdom and knowledge are always open.*'

Louise Hay